THE STURGIS EXPERIENCE

A CELEBRATION OF THE BLACK HILLS MOTORCYCLE RALLY

BY JIM CASEY

PHOTOGRAPHS BY SEAN BOWE

RUNNING PRESS

PHILADELPHIA · LONDON

Printed in China

This book may not be reproduced in whole or in part, in any form or by any means, electronic or mechanical, including photocopying, recording, or by any information storage and retrieval system now known or hereafter invented, without written permission from the publisher.

Library of Congress Control Number 2003110221

ISBN 0-7624-1883-4

9   8   7   6   5   4   3   2   1
Digit on the right indicates the number of this printing

Cover and interior design: Dustin Summers
Photo editor: Susan Oyama
Edited by: Keltie Hawkins

Cover and interior photographs by Sean Bowe, copyrighted by the photographer.
For information on the photographs of Sean Bowe, please contact the photographer
at (303)449-3906.

Photographs on pp. 17, 23, 37, 47, 53, 70, and 75 by © Basil Snyman, D.C.

Black Hills Motorcycle Rally patches reproduced by permission of the Jackpine Gypsies
http://www.jackpine-gypsies.com.

This book may be ordered by mail from the publisher.
But try your bookstore first!

Published by Courage Books, an imprint of
Running Press Book Publishers
125 South Twenty-second Street
Philadelphia, Pennsylvania 19103-4399

Visit us on the web!
www.runningpress.com

There are many people who made this dream come true:

Rolph, without who there would be no such book, and who put the mess into order for me. Keltie, who is a saint and definitely my favorite editor. Brian, who was so willing to go beyond and above, and to read all the crude drafts I put in front of him. To professor Carl Edeman, without who there could have been no real history section. H.S. Thompson and the other pioneers of motorcycle journalism. A nod to Dan Hartman who gave me my first real job doing this stuff, along with Troy Johnson who allowed me to take my first staggering steps.

Thanks should always be given to all the educational professionals out there, and I am deeply indebted to those who have been there for me along the way. Manic Kim, Smilin' Tim and Long Tall Chuck who have kept my chin up, and for that they are true blue bros.

And finally, I wish to acknowledge the life of excellence lived by Pearl Hoel. She should be an inspiration to us all.

THIS BOOK IS DEDICATED TO CINDY, MUM, AND GRAMMY. THE THREE WOMEN IN MY LIFE—

THE ROCK, THE SUPPORT, AND THE INSPIRATION. OH, AND TO HANK, THE BUDDY, TOO.

WELCOME RIDERS BANNER, MAIN STREET, STURGIS, 2003

CONTENTS

This trip to Sturgis, like all trips to Sturgis, was

about doing my own thing. But somehow over

the recent years, I had become less sure of what

my own thing was. Times had changed, and I

begrudgingly had to admit that I had changed

too. Age will do that to you. Yet, we all want to

think of ourselves as the same person we were

in our twenties or even teens. Experience and

time chip away at that innocence.

I leaned down hard on my gear one more time to cinch down the straps. I got about one more inch out of the tie-down. I stepped back to examine the balance of my load. The old black duffel bag was firmly cinched to the rear rack, which I had just put on. My sleeping bag and tent were fastened to my handlebars. Comfort taken in old rituals.

The sun was still slung low in the sky. I had been up since dark. Now the light was cracking through the pine trees, throwing a glow upon the dew on my lawn. My footprints were solid imprints in the dew. When I squinted my eyes, the dew became a million tiny spectrums of light and color.

I lit a cigarette and caught the drift of a Willie Nelson tape that was playing in the garage: "I know just what I'd change/ If I could go back in time somehow/ But there's nothing I could do about it now." I smiled, and caught myself nodding vaguely.

Blackallac stood in the driveway ready to go. Ready for the trip to Sturgis. She was a 1992 FLHS, stripped down tight, and low to the ground. I had always preferred stripped bikes. On her, I had lowered the front end an inch and a half and the back three. I had a large custom solo seat that had the texture and essence of a Western saddle. The rear fender stood out, looking like one huge, single unit with the fiberglass saddlebags. Instead of chrome (the opiate of the modern biker), I had done the casings and the carb cover in anodized black. The pipes came out of her black heart like chrome arteries, flaring at the back into unbaffled fishtails. She was big and black. She was Blackallac.

I watched my smoke drift up and fade away. I was forty-one years old. I had spent the last twenty-five years biking. I was a biker. At one time that had a concise meaning. It seemed to have less now, as time has gone by.

PAUL COX GLANCES BACK AS HE RIDES HIS HAND-BUILT, LEATHER-COVERED CHOPPER, NEAR BEAR BUTTE, STURGIS, 2003

In a biker text book, *Zen and the Art of Motorcycle Maintenance*, Robert Pirsig had a pretty good take on time. In the Western model, the future is out before you. And the past is behind you. He points out that, in Asian philosophy, the future comes from behind. It is unseeable, and the past is fading away before your eyes. That is the way I see time. Or the way I don't see time perhaps. I have no idea what the future bears. These kinds of musings have always brought more than my share of kidding from my bros. They like to call me an egghead. But never in front of "civilians." To me and my riding buddies, a civilian is anyone who lives outside the brotherhood. Anyone who is not absolutely committed to our way of life.

Albert Camus, the existentialist novelist, said, "An intellectual is someone whose mind watches itself." I liked that. If you're not watching your own mind, you aren't controlling what it absorbs. And if that's the case, you are nothing more than a sponge, soaking up someone else's agenda.

This trip to Sturgis, like all trips to Sturgis, was about doing my own thing. But somehow over the recent years, I had become less sure of what my own thing was. Times had changed, and I begrudgingly had to admit that I had changed too. Age will do that to you. Yet, we all want to think of ourselves as the same person we were in our twenties or even teens. Experience and time chip away at that innocence.

Thinking about time, watching the smoke drift away, I remembered my first conscious experience with motorcycles and bikers. I was with my old man, driving down the freeway. I suppose I was seven years old. From behind us came a tremendous roar, like a tornado. I rolled down the window, and stuck my head out, into the rushing wind. As my face caught the

wind, the first bike flashed by—so fast and fierce it seemed like a blow to the head. Then came one after another, two abreast. Mechanical flashes of lightning. As the last pair flew by, I pulled my head in, and managed to catch sight of the words written in red on their backs: "Hells Angels."

"What does that mean, Dad, Hells Angels?" I asked.

"It means they are a bunch of losers," he said, his shoulders hunched up around his ears, red-faced and white-knuckled. Same as he always looked: pissed, angry, disappointed. But I knew my dad was dead wrong. To me they were gods: riding roaring, snorting, maniacal steeds. And I wanted to be one of them.

Growing up, I had no doubt that I was going to get a motorcycle the minute I could. We would pull it off, me and Buddha, my best friend and riding partner for the next twenty-five years. We met when we were thirteen, and he was kind of chubby. He had a habit of saying weird cryptic stuff. Even then he spent hours reading the Upanishads and other works of Asian philosophy. I think he started out thinking that it would increase his appeal to certain girls. But it didn't seem to, and pretty soon it just became a part of who he was. I was the one who dubbed him Buddha; that also just became a part of who he was.

As a teenager, I had no interest in Buddha's philosophical spoutings. They had nothing to do with my obsession: motorcycles. His natural, incessant, and overpowering curiosity about life allowed him to be more even-keeled than I was. My bedroom was full of pin-up bikes from any source I could get my hands on. When I discovered a biker magazine that came out every month, it became my bible. Dozens of hours of schoolwork were lost as I daydreamed and drew pictures of the bikes that I would someday create.

Buddha scored first. He'd heard about an old Triumph that belonged to one of his grandfather's friends. It was stored in the old guy's shed. A '54 TRS Trophy. It was a rigid frame with a solo seat. Chrome and silver paint. To us, it was the First Wonder of the World. His grandfather helped us get it home. We manhandled it into the back of Gramps' pickup, all three of us covered in dirt and bird crap by the time we were finished. We pulled into his driveway with the basket case. His mother hovered around us like we had brought the devil himself to her house.

"I just don't know. I just don't know," she said. Since Buddha's dad had split when Buddha was ten, she was perpetually turned out like she was off to the Ladies Garden Club. I don't know whether it was a device to attract a new man, or to compensate for the blow to her fragile ego when he left. But she was definitely broken and smelled of gin. She was a nervous, finch-like woman: neurotic, twitchy, and brightly colored. Her pretensions of middle-class respectability ended with that bike. The vanishing of a husband was one thing, a biker son another.

"Listen Alice," said Gramps. "He's about grown, and he could use something like this to get him away from all those goofy books. He's gonna be a man. It will give him character." To me, it made him look like a tough guy. That's what character meant in our neighborhood. It had nothing to do with virtue or duty or obligation, traditional hallmarks of character. Righteousness was a guy who took no lip, stood up for himself and his family, and never backed away from a confrontation. To do so was to be marked as weak, and you might as well paint a bull's-eye on your forehead. Most of the neighborhood guys were "macho," but tough was more than an exterior quality; it had to do with your interior, your guts.

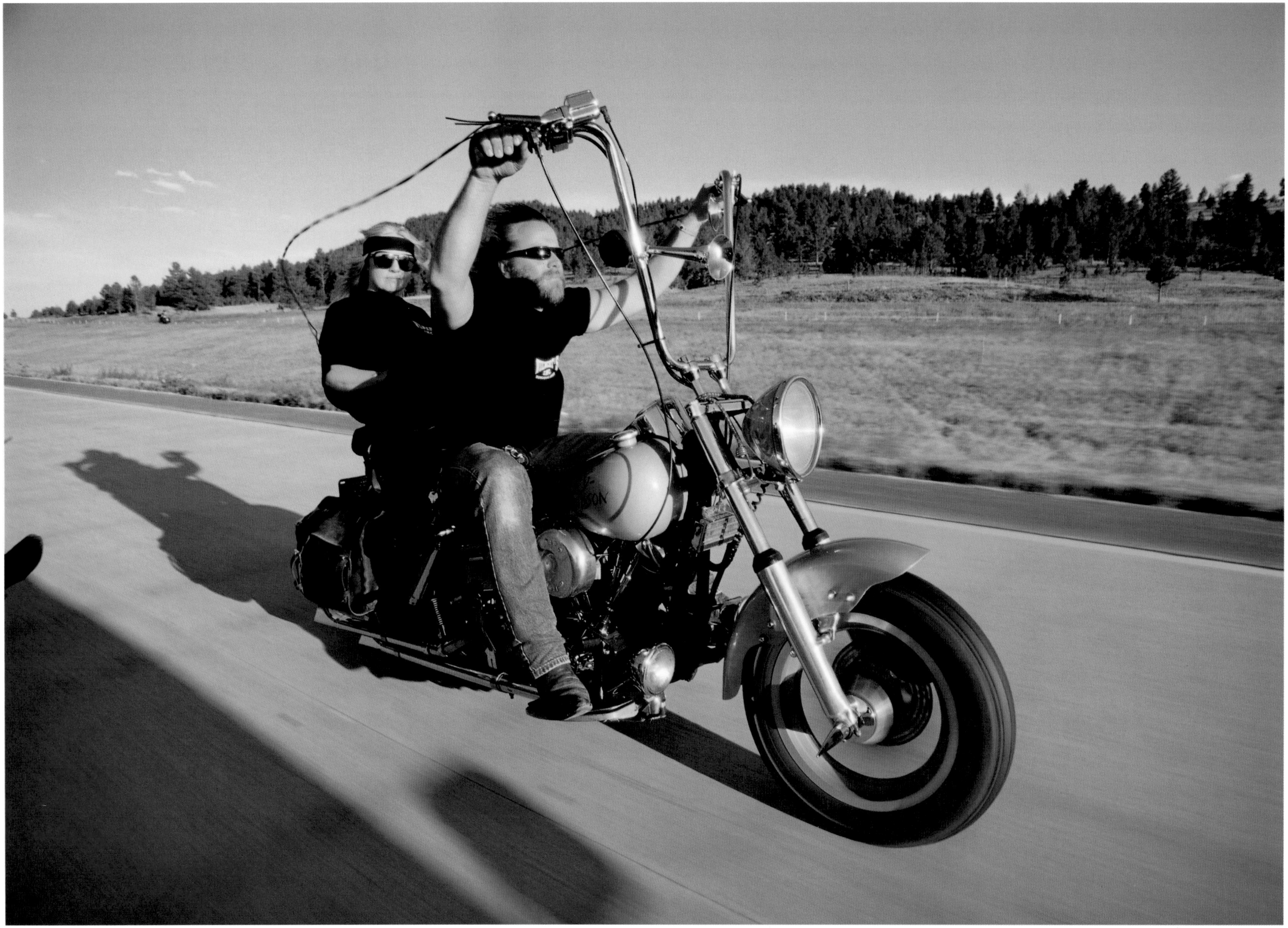

JOE TRACY ON HIS HIGH BAR SHOVELHEAD, STURGIS, 1994

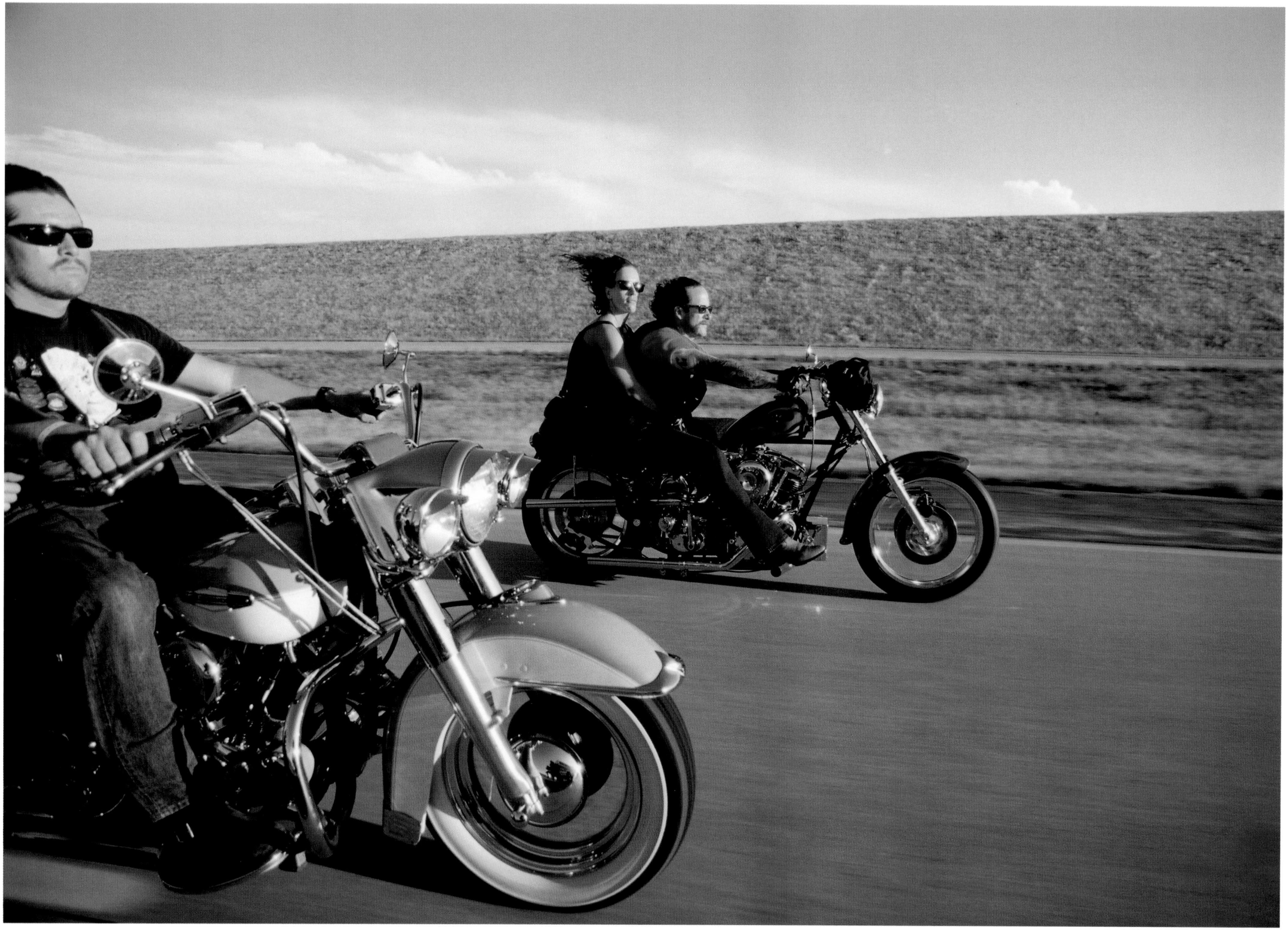

RIDING THE INTERSTATE DURING THE STURGIS RALLY, 1994

The majority of us got kicked around by our old men when we were young. It affected our attitudes toward violence. It also affected our attitudes toward authority. We disrespected it. When it came in the form of a belligerent, violent drunk, it affected your outlook on all authority from that point on. Authority is something that is earned and not demanded.

We weren't afraid of violence. It lost that scary dimension of the unknown factor. And once you got to a certain point, you decided not to take it any more and you fought back. Fighting a full-grown man is a big confidence builder. You know you can take it. Violence can be a part of the biker lifestyle. It is a part of life, not the lifestyle. I have never looked for a fight, but I have never backed away from one either.

I stubbed out my cigarette and went into the garage to grab a diaper. A couple of times a year I bought a few dozen of them. They were perfect for cleaning bikes. I went back to Blackallac and wiped down all the surfaces. I always insisted on starting out a journey with a spotless bike. An hour out she would have gathered some dirt, but that didn't matter. Polishing a bike was a matter of biker pride. I had known some of the grubbiest, crustiest, foulest guys on Earth that would never dream of setting out on a dirty bike.

It was one of the many rituals, the nuances of what Buddha and I had long ago deemed "This Thing of Ours." I suppose we first heard it in *The Godfather* or something like that. "La Cosa Nostra." We knew we weren't Mafia types, but the term seemed to fit perfectly. We were completely committed to values of brotherhood, and willing to do just about anything to live the life we had dreamed of.

Before we even had bikes, we had adopted the symbols of the biker. Long hair, black T-shirts, jeans, leather jackets, and engineer boots. Heavy belts made out of bike chains and skin. An extended fork, king-queen seat, a half-assed chopper. A that itched to be inked. No designer labels, even genuine Harley T-shirts were rare. A "Dickies" T-shirt was as close as we got. For the most part, "biker chicks" just dressed in jeans and black tees and leather jackets. No engineer boots, mostly moon shoes or waffle boots. No one was making the feminized version of biker fashion back then. Or any fashionable version of biker fashion. Our gear was simple and had meaning; it wasn't a costume one put on, it was a statement. A line in the sand to be defended with fists and feet, mind's volition and soul.

Buddha and I were working-class kids. In these times, one is not supposed to delineate between the classes. It might make someone feel like they don't belong. The thing is you don't have to tell someone they don't belong—they already know it in their heart, and some choose to wear it on their sleeves.

The better-off dads had trades, the rest remained on the fringes of the labor market. We knew that other kids' mothers would never dream of having jobs, not staying at home. Most of our mothers worked in factories, or laundries, something like that. Going to school with solid, middle-class kids alienated us. Our mothers seemed old before their time and our dads were angry, bitter guys who manhandled us in a boozy haze at the slightest provocation, real or imagined.

We were different. We were going to create a different reality. We were going to escape the jobs on the fringe, and the existence that had seemed to stomp the dreams out of neighborhood guys who were still young. Escape on our motorcycles. They were our one-way tickets out.

My first bike was a real bastard and was bought on the day I got my permit on my fifteenth birthday—a Honda 750, with an extended fork, king-queen seat, a half-assed chopper. A Harley was still out of my price range, and at the time I didn't care what I got; I just had to own a bike. I had ferreted away a few hundred bucks, hustling. I met the seller in the ally, behind his garage. I was so rattled with apprehension, I could barely hold it together as I straddled the sled. I fought to steady my nerves and kicked her over. I had exaggerated my riding experience when I talked to the guy over the phone. It actually amounted to a few rides around the block on Buddha's bike. In a stupid burst of speed, I took off like a wildman down to the end of the alley, which teed onto a busy street. Just before I hit the intersection, I went to brake and immediately downshifted instead. Lodged between the apehangers, ass pointed up in the air, I managed to downshift one more time before I shot across the street and into the curb. I was thrown onto the sidewalk, my feet having looped over my head, and the bike was in the street. The throttle was stuck, so the damn thing lay on its side and spun around and around, engine screaming in the high rev range the whole time. I managed to accidentally hit the kill switch, trying to grab the whirling machine as my legs were knocked from under me. Looking up from my seat in the middle of the street, a crowd had gathered to witness my humiliation. Word of my encounter with the doughnutting, riderless machine had spread, and within a few days I became known as "Crash," a moniker that has stuck to this day. Most people I know couldn't even tell you my real name.

Buddha and I rode the living hell out of those bikes. Come Friday afternoon, we were long gone. A sleeping bag and ten or

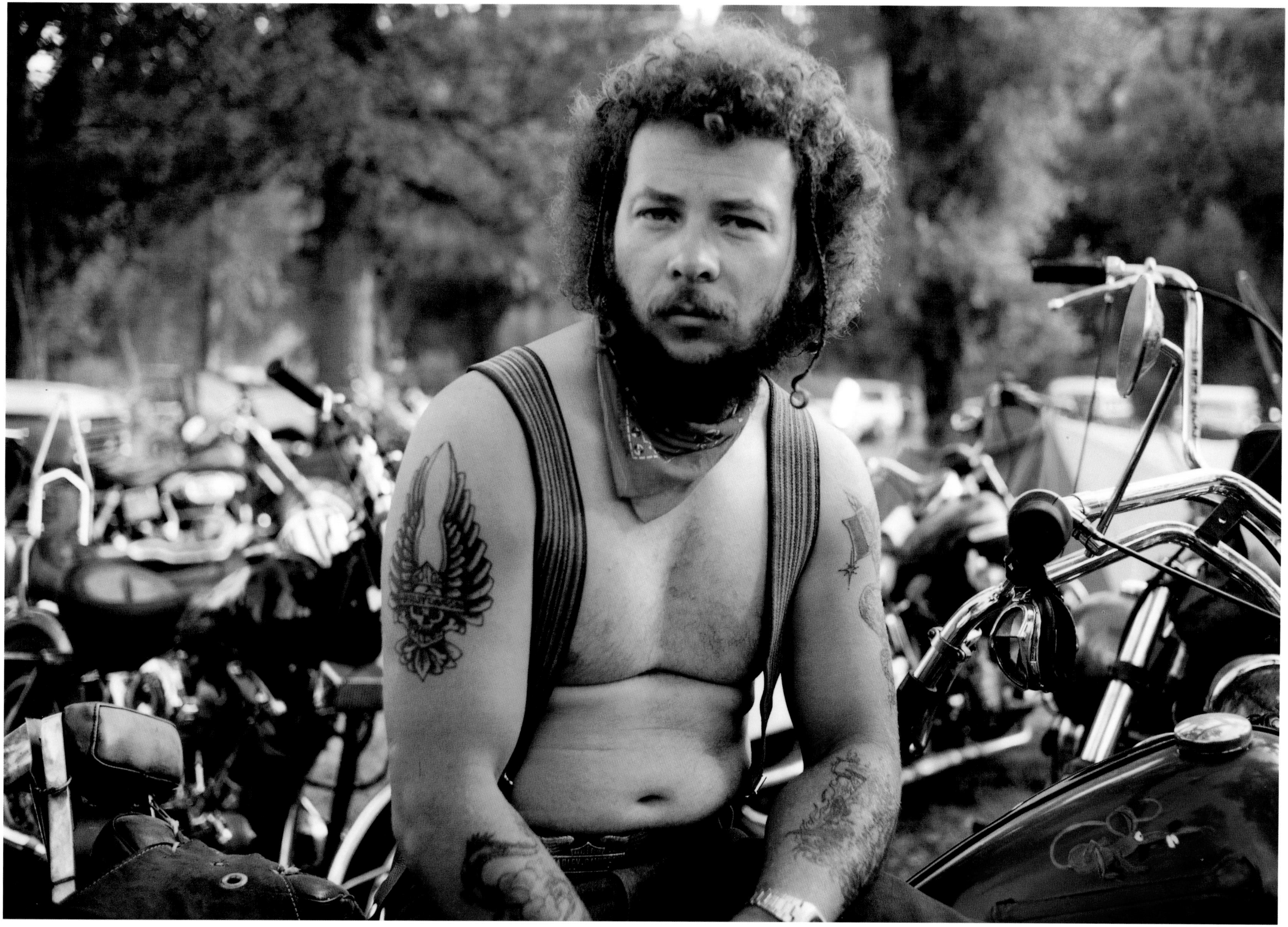

IDAHO CAMPER, CITY PARK, STURGIS, 1980

twenty bucks, that was it. It was a four-hour ride to the state line, where the legal drinking age was 18, and we could easily buy beer. We learned every back road, many not even on the map. We were the Lewis and Clark of low-budget motorcycles. At the drive-ins and other teenage hangouts, we were kings. The bikes assured us a stream of admiring girls. The guys mostly ignored us—or pretended they did.

We were little Brando and Kerouac clichés back then. Like anyone who is just finding out who they really are, we were obvious. The funny thing is, though I think we are all born different, we learn to be the same. As the years went by, we learned that "This Thing of Ours" was about having heart and living honestly, refusing to bend to the inevitable grind of conformity. But today, standing in the driveway, I had lost the abandon, the fervor of the early years. The risk-taking that had brought all the rewards. I felt old and washed out.

I took a deep breath, inhaling the morning air. For the first time I was anxious about this trip to Sturgis. I closed and locked my garage door, the pink and orange gone from the morning sky. The last thing I did before taking off was to put on my chaps. I had them custom-made years ago, out in Portland, Oregon, by a guy who gave you a lifetime guarantee. They were wiped down and oiled, something I only did a couple of times a year. Most of the time they were bug-covered. Grasshopper heads, staring out like the miniature heads of mounted game.

I walked over to the bike, turned the petcock and hit start. I have never lost the thrill of starting a Harley-Davidson. That first ear-splitting crack as the engine catches life and breathes fire. The ritual of adjusting the choke to get her just right, pounding out the right tempo. Lifting up the kickstand, I cracked the throttle, rolled down the driveway and out on to the road, making a hard, graceful arc right, clinging to control what has always seemed like a barely controllable beast. Riding a bike feels a lot like living life at full throttle.

It had been nine years since I had been to Sturgis, a major slice of life. Before that, I had made five other trips, spread out over a dozen years or so. In the years since my last trip, I had made plans to return, plans that always seemed to fall apart, subjugated to the demands of everyday life.

I was setting out on a journey, a journey to Sturgis, to recapture what felt like a life lost. Not an unusual activity for a man of forty-one. I had lived a life full of bikes, wild sex, and wilder parties. I had no need for a Corvette or any other symbol of midlife crisis. What I was in search of was more spiritual. Not in the religious sense, more as in searching for the essence of an earlier time: a time when things seemed more obvious, more black and white. When a biker was a biker, with the distinct meaning that it held. A box of beliefs and codes. A total way of life. But none of us are any one thing; we are a totality, cut into pieces, like a puzzle. Often who we think we are, or how we like to see ourselves, is a portion of that complete picture. But those romanticized visions of ourselves are really minute pieces of who we are.

Like myself, like many others, Sturgis had transformed over the years, had matured, lost its innocence and wild abandon. Had more rules, more civilized codes of behavior. Had become commercial and more about the money. Sturgis seemed to be a reflection of mostly everyone I knew. Yet, I knew that the essence of the original Sturgis, and the Sturgis of the seventies and early eighties was still present. In the event, and in all of us who attend. My journey was to find that Sturgis, to seek it out in others, and to confirm that I was still the person that I believed myself to be.

By late afternoon, I reached the Great Plains. I'm cruising at about eighty-five miles an hour. Fast enough to dig the speed, yet slow enough to absorb the character of the landscape. On either side of the old two-laner, soft green hills rolled out toward the horizon, overlapping and layered. Empiricism is the belief that all we learn, that all we know, comes from our senses. If that's the case, then traveling in the wind must give you a much greater appreciation of all that you encounter.

I am unable to ride these spaces without feeling an appreciation for the pioneers who traipsed through here, looking for a new life. I think most bikers have a special feel for the Western spaces and the people that opened them up. It's a form of cultural memory: an attraction to the cowboy, that Great American folk hero. There isn't a biker alive who hasn't seen himself as an outlaw cowboy, wandering the land on his faithful steed.

And in many ways, bikers are the last real American folk heroes: the last free spirits to wander the open spaces looking for adventure, looking to leave life's petty constraints behind. The American cowboy is the greatest of all folk heroes, trading a life of low wages and hardships for freedom and individual pride. The antithesis of material pursuit.

And from the age of sixteen to thirty-two, that's exactly what Buddha and I did; we dedicated ourselves to living out a

cowboyish, *Easy Rider* life, and reveled in the contradictions that the terms and the lifestyle contained. Life on the road is often hard. Throwing yourself into the wind is like strapping yourself to a catapult, cutting the rope, and blasting into time and space, never knowing where you are going to end up.

For almost twenty years we lived between working to scrape up traveling money and being on the road. Even our periods of working, having apartments and bills to pay, were chaotic. We'd skip out on our rent and put false names on utility bills, phone bills, and the like. Dodging around avoiding the yoke of normal responsibility. After high school we'd gone to trade school, having seen the difference between the guys with trades and those who tried to make a go of it with no skills. Weekdays spent in school, weekends in search of bacchanal affairs, winding highways, and scrapes with straights.

We'd traveled close to 500,000 miles in those years, almost exclusively out West. We avoided interstates almost as much as the highway patrolmen. We'd ride together, sometimes alone, and often with an ever-changing pack. Stand-up folks who lived and breathed the lifestyle. People you never doubted would back your next move, let you flop at their place, or would bail you out literally or figuratively. We juxtaposed our bizarre order of normalcy against a straight lifestyle, the overlap often the basis of crazy, true adventures.

Buddha's inquiry into matters of spirit and philosophy had drawn me in. Woven through our journeys was a soundtrack from the great books of philosophy, Eastern and less often, Western. Hundreds of nights around a fire, in the wilderness, flashlights trained on the pages of the great books of knowledge. Kant and *Siddhartha* ingested while slapping at mosquitoes.

Often read out loud, a message allowed to drift outward, upward, following the campfire smoke into the cosmos. Daytime spent with the pounding background of unbaffled, V-twin engines.

I've come to see life as an accumulation of all one's journeys traveled. And your life's journeys connect to all that went before you, beside you, and ahead of you. Thousands of lives, thousands of journeys bound together, like a great rope, winding through the cosmos. As I travel, I am a part of that rope, attempting to follow, to stay true to my own strand.

And here I was, crossing the plains, once more on the road, after an absence of ten years. Years spent building a home, selling it, and building more, going to school, aware of the ticking clock's sweeping hands, not wanting to spend my old age with nothing. Trying to attain that which many of the straights already had. My riding was suddenly restricted to long weekends, none of the extended trips to places such as Sturgis. I wanted to find the strands that connected me to this grand event.

VISITOR CENTER STUDY OF THE CRAZY HORSE MONUMENT, WITH CARVED MONUMENT IN THE DISTANCE, BLACK HILLS, SOUTH DAKOTA, 1996

Time present and time past

Are both perhaps present in time future,

And time future contained in time past.

If all time is eternally present

All time is unredeemable.

What might have been is an abstraction

Remaining a perpetual possibility

Only in a world of speculation.

—T.S. Eliot, "Burnt Norton"

Hundreds of millions of years ago, the Black Hills stood above an inland sea. A sea full of strange life forms, giant jawed fish, and sightless tubes with waving flanges. Today the Black Hills can be seen at a great distance, rising dark from the Great Prairie. At least once a year, they again become inhabited with strange life forms. The modern day Partyous Bikerous.

The Lakota Sioux believed the Hills to be sacred. As if they were a pure, essential form of nature. Early white visitors included the legendary likes of Jeremiah Johnson, the wild, tough, bearded mountain man. By the 1870s the white man was itching to get a hold of the Hills, based upon the rumors of the great veins of gold and other natural resources that were submerged in the oasis-like Hills that rose from the plains.

George Armstrong Custer, with his long hair and well-doc-umented lack of impulse control, busted the Hills wide open. Although they were promised to the natives in the Fort Laramie Treaty of 1868, "as long as the grass grows and the water flows," the Hills were swarming with white men as soon as Custer got his butt kicked over in southeast Montana. Gamblers, prostitutes, and con men were partying along with the crusty miners, the beady-eyed gunmen, and the broken, drunken town Indians who lived on the fringes. Walk the streets of any of the Black Hills towns, and with only a small imagination, one can smell the cheap perfume of the ladies and the bodies of the miners.

Some of these early pioneers stayed, most moved on to the next boom town. Those who stayed behind kept their firmly guarded independent natures. The modern inhabitants are the direct descendants of these sturdy souls, in nature if not by genetics.

In 1976, Buddha and I saw *Easy Rider* at a midnight show-

JAMMIN' TO MT. RUSHMORE, SOUTH DAKOTA, 2002

THROUGH THE TUNNEL, NEEDLES HIGHWAY, NEAR MOUNT RUSHMORE, SOUTH DAKOTA, 2003

ing. Bikes were lined up and down the block, hot chrome and wild paint glowing in the streetlights. The line for tickets looked like some kind of black caterpillar, as leather-clad guys and chicks slouched against the brick wall. We were sure that every square passing by saw us as a band of half-human hoodlums. We relished the fact. Beers and bottles of cheap wine were passed back and forth, the air perfumed with the sweet scent of Colombian Gold. Man, were we jazzed. We were with our people, our tribe. We were the anti-Christ to the squares who spent their time in stale jobs, material wealth their only god. We were not outsiders that night. We were ultimate insiders, hip to and bearers of truth. We were gathered together to watch the masterpiece that was the protest against the world of devious squares.

About 3:30 that morning, we were in the last group of bikes to be driven from the street by the cops. Buddha ended up leading a group of about ten bikes up into the Hills. The moon was full, high in a star-spangled sky. Suddenly he braked hard, causing several bikes behind him to lock up their brakes. He jumped off his bike in the middle of the deserted road, unable to contain himself for a second longer. He hit the button on a tape recorder strapped to his bike and Steppenwolf's "Born to Be Wild" split the morning sky. We all jumped off the bikes, about fifteen of us, and started dancing wildly. A half-mad groove, fueled by the intoxicating freedom of youth. The song ended and there was a minute of total silence, as each one of us gulped the frigid morning air. We were kings in that moment, kings of a world dedicated to freedom and devoid of squares. For each one of us, it was as good as life got. But for me and Buddha, having our bikes was no longer enough. We were gonna be saddle tramps, man. Easy Riders. Endless Easy Riders.

My senior year in high school, I got my chance to taste what I craved. It was November. I'd polished off Thanksgiving dinner and decided to top off the evening by going out riding with Furb, my mother's brother, a biker to the bone who was rarely invited to family functions. Even though I had only been riding for a couple of years, I was on my third bike. A Vincent with a dubious title. It was like riding a 150-mile-an-hour pogo stick. About five miles into the ride, Furb suggested we trade off. I knew that Furb never let a single soul touch his bike. I couldn't believe that he was going to let me ride it. His permission made it one of the biggest moments of my life. I approached his chopped Panhead, my heart rattling like a machine gun. I kicked the beast to life and felt like every sense in my body was going to overload and cause my head to explode. Twenty miles later, I got off, an addicted man, condemned to a life of V-twins and oil leaks.

The story of Harley-Davidson is the story of a company battling with adversity. Struggling to do it their way. A story in which the heroes make almost fatal mistakes and then redeem themselves by struggling back to their roots. The company fought extinction as the world changed all around them, and won, doing it their way. This spirit is part of what infuses each machine with a spirit of freedom. The story of Harley is the story of the biker, and the story of Sturgis.

The Harley and Davidson founders had started out with motorized bicycles. By 1903, they could see the future of transportation, and made the first Harley-Davidson motorcycle. It was a 405cc, leather loop-driven marvel. This first marvel wasn't

INTERSTATE 90, NEAR THE WYOMING–SOUTH DAKOTA STATE LINE, 1999

for sale; it was built to satisfy their own craving for speed and adrenaline. It was of such superior quality, several people lined up for their own. With a couple of deposits in their pockets, they were in business, grasping the American dream. One of them painted the words Harley-Davidson Motor Co. over the door, and a legend was born.

During this time, many other young men were building their backyard version of this new thing, the motorcycle. About three hundred different manufacturers were working to put out a bike. Most of them failed quickly, as they had poor designs and crummy engineering. They were proving that attaching a motor to a flimsy bicycle frame did not a motorcycle make. The HD boys were building a product with a rugged frame and forks tough enough to take the stresses of the larger-than-average engines. The bikes had an instant reputation for being over-engineered, weighty, and possessing overkill in the engine. But, in endurance competitions, they were indomitable. The second bike they ever made was still running after a 100,000 miles and a couple of owners. Within five years Harley was putting out 450 machines a year from a small factory that had replaced the garden shed. These early models became known as the "Silent Grey Fellows," and were the standard for the fledgling industry. By World War I, the American bike market was dominated by two manufacturers, Harley and Indian. During the war, Indian dedicated their entire production to military bikes while Harley maintained a consumer market. One day after the Armistice in 1918, a young corporal from Chippewa Falls, Wisconsin, was the first American to enter Germany. He was riding a Harley-Davidson motorcycle. Motorcycles were a more popular form of personal transportation during that time than the automobile.

In 1920, Harley produced 28,189 motorcycles, which were shipped to sixty-nine different countries. In 1921, Ford only produced 10,202 cars.

During the teens and twenties, Harley produced a 1000cc engine. In 1929, they produced the 45-inch (750cc), which was a constant for 45 years. The year, 1929 instantly sparks recognition as the year of the stock market crash. That year, Harley production was a healthy 22,350 units. By the following year, production shrank. By '34 Harley was barely staying alive with a total production of 3,703 units. As the United States struggled to emerge from the Depression, Harley continued to struggle as well. In '36 they began production of the Knucklehead. This model had fifty percent more power and set a land speed record of 136 mph. While this model went a long way to increasing Harley's share of the market, the company continued to struggle, along with the rest of the American economy and the American people.

In 1935, Harley-Davidson made a move that would eventually change motorcycling forever. They started the Japanese motorcycling industry when they sold Sankyo Co. licenses for blueprints, tools, dies, and machinery. This was the first Japanese company and was called Rikuo Motorcycle. This was the beginning of an industry that would eventually threaten the very existence of Harley some twenty-five years later. The Japanese would make them cheaper and produce better technology than Harley would ever produce.

Prior to World War II, almost all bikes sold in the United States were American-made. Harley thrived during the war as a major supplier to the war effort. Like many of the brave men on the battlefront, Harley won a few medals. In 1943, they earned the first of their "E" awards for excellence. Many of the U.S.

RIDING THROUGH THE RAIN, BOULDER CANYON, NEAR DEADWOOD, SOUTH DAKOTA, 1995

servicemen were exposed to Harleys during the war, an effect that was important to the survival of Harley after the war, and to the creation of the "biker."

After the war, Harley lost ground to British bikes such as Triumph and Norton, which were cheaper—and 20 mph faster—than Harleys. American motorcycles had enjoyed the protection of huge tariffs during the Great Depression. As a part of the Marshall Plan, these tariffs were lifted, and the Brits began a substantial attack on the American market. Their technology was simply better, and the machines easier to control with the foot shifter, which did away with the clumsy "suicide-clutch" arrangement.

Indian Motorcycles had been less successful than Harley in obtaining government contracts. Prior to the war, Indian was family-owned, as well as being the first American production bike. During and after the war they were bought out by a corporation and seemed to lose heart. They spent most of the war supplying spare parts for other machines. After the war, they were never able to regain the solid footing they had previously enjoyed. In the early fifties, they were absorbed by a British company and, within a few years, were extinct.

1948 saw the birth of the Panhead, which was a somewhat successful effort to solve overheating and lubrication problems. The Panhead ushered in the booming fifties. Although the fifties was a time of almost unprecedented economic growth, it was also a time that saw the demise of Harley's chief American rival, Indian. Harley was the sole survivor of three-hundred-plus American motorcycle companies. On top of that unexpected boon, Harley gained some priceless publicity when rock 'n rollers like Elvis were seen and photographed on their own

Harleys. Under attack by the British, Harley made changes in suspension, and eventually the shifter. Younger riders wanted to go faster, with the greater ease of a hand clutch and foot shift that were offered on the Brit bikes. The company managed to hold on to a fiercely loyal crowd that demanded an American V-twin engine, imparting the feeling of nostalgia—offering the opportunity to ride the land and remember kindred souls and times gone by.

By the sixties, the Japanese were launching an attack on the American bike market. With their small, high-revving engines, it is doubtful that they were competing with Harley for the same rider. The two groups of consumers were breeds apart. An example of what was considered a giant technological change on a Harley was the electric start that appeared on the '65 "Electra-Glide," a Panhead that was changed to the Shovelhead the following year. The Japanese motorcycle industry,

which Harley had been responsible for creating back in the twenties, was surging forward, marketing to the young, clean-cut, middle-class crowd who saw the motorcycle as a dynamic toy. Honda was a winner during this period with their slogan: "You meet the nicest people on a Honda." Naturally this slogan can be read to mean that the nice people are on the Honda, or that when on a Honda, you meet nice people. The campaign was a subtle dig at the public's new consciousness of the outlaw Harley rider.

The market at large was symbolic of a change in American spirit, juxtapositions of a youth market that craved speed and inexpensive machines, against the traditionalist V-twin rider that craved nothing more than a loud, snorting cruise on a traditional American bike. These latter riders were a minority, as Harley's market share had shrunk to six percent. These were bleak days at Harley headquarters, and only a miracle or some kind of dynamic shift in culture could save the HOG from extinction.

THREE BIKES RIDE INTERSTATE 90, WEST OF STURGIS, 1984

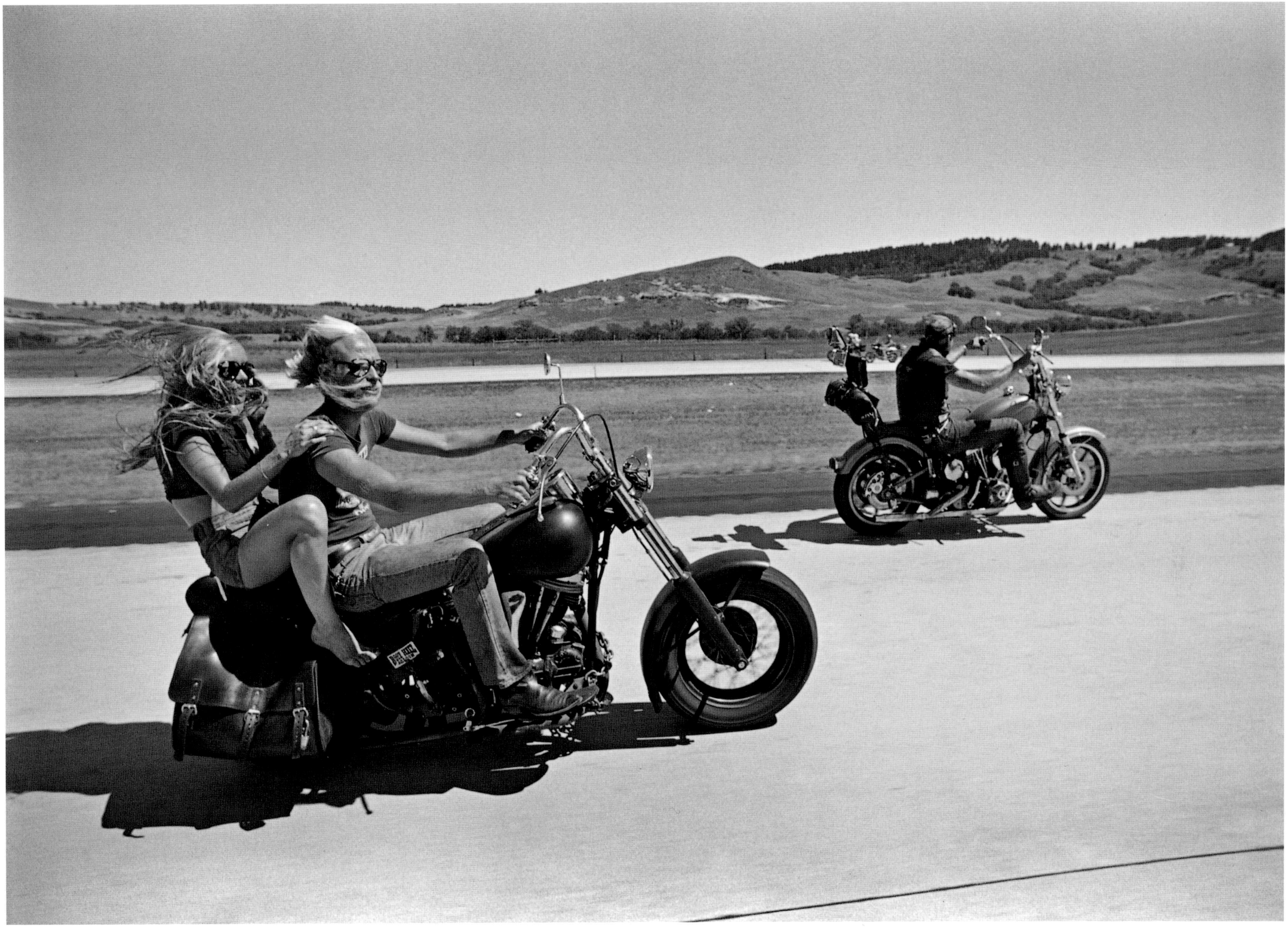

IN THE WIND, INTERSTATE 90, WHITEWOOD, SOUTH DAKOTA, 1984

T he image of the motorcyclist of the pre-war era was not the same picture that emerged after the war. While there is no doubt that there may have been a few loutish, beer-guzzling hellraisers who lived to drag race their bikes, for the most part, the cycle enthusiast of the time was a clean-cut stand-up citizen with an equally well-scrubbed gal on the back. The stereotypical outfit of the day was a cop-style hat, a few destination pins attached to a brown leather jacket with a dark fur collar, loose pants, possibly even a pair of jodhpurs, and knee-high riding boots. In fact, the average enthusiast looked almost identical to the motorcycle cops who covered the land. Looking back at archival photos, it would seem that many enthusiasts were even prone to wearing neckties while scooting around.

The war provided a major cultural change that was to have a huge, long-term impact on the motorcycling scene. Many of the returning GIs were introduced to American V-twins while serving overseas. Upon their return stateside, many ex-servicemen chose to stay in California, where they had been discharged. This left a large population of young men in a booming economy settling back into normal life. The expectation was that they should marry, perhaps go to college on the GI bill, and raise their families, while working away at good jobs. However, many of these ex-servicemen had spent a considerable part of the last few years being shot at and shooting back. Veterans of high stress and connoisseurs of adrenaline-charged high times. Settling back into a "normal" lifestyle was to prove more than difficult for many.

Many began to seek release in the most dangerous and thrilling—yet still legal—thing out there. The big American

California has long been the birthplace of various subcultures: surfing, hot-rodding, Beats, and hippies. It also gave birth to the biker and bikerism. In the mid-forties, groups of the aforementioned vets started forming cycle clubs.

These clubs consisted of guys who got together on the weekends to ride around the countryside, drink some beer, and blow off steam.

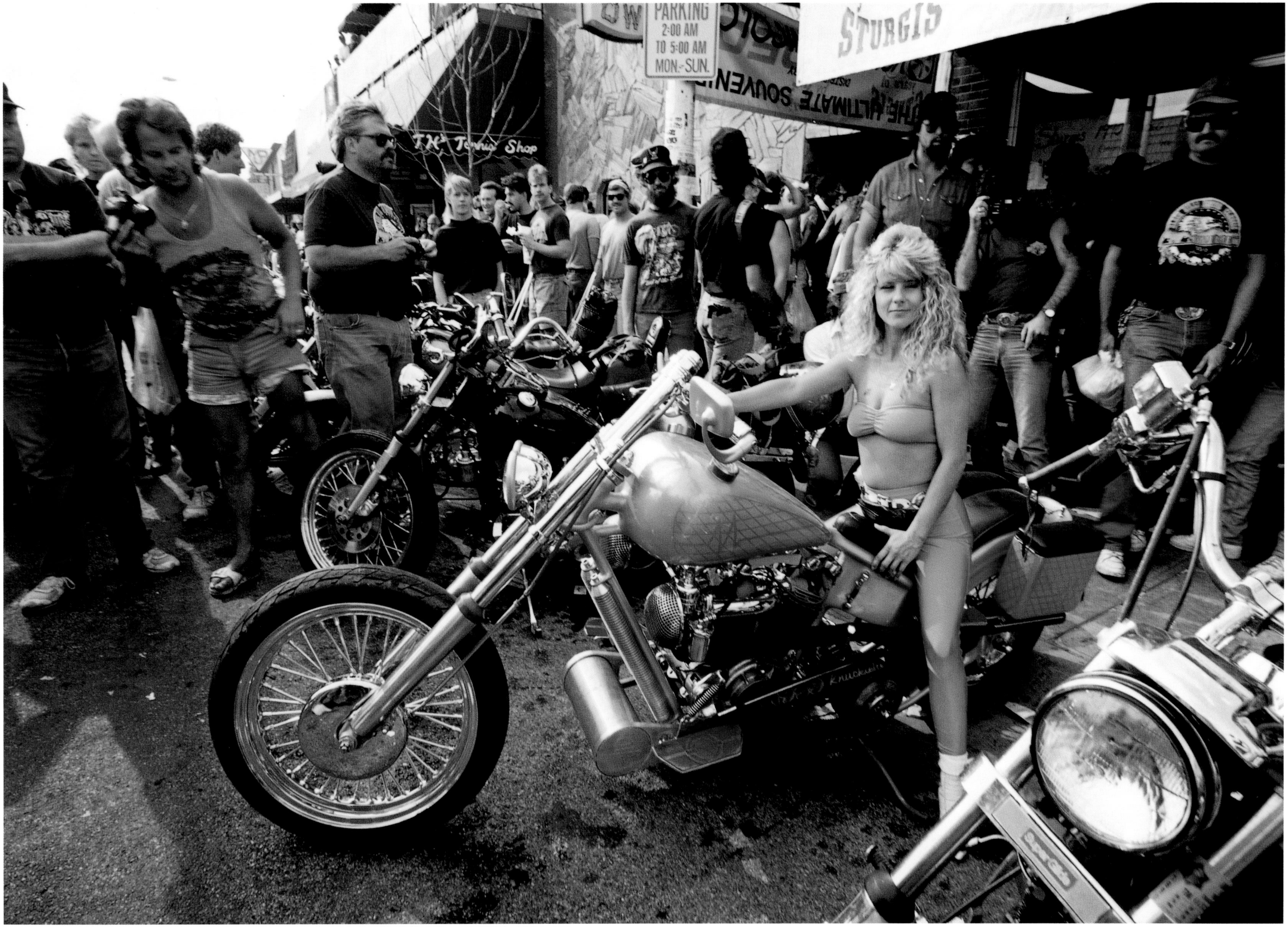

POSING ON BLUE, MAIN STREET, STURGIS, 1990

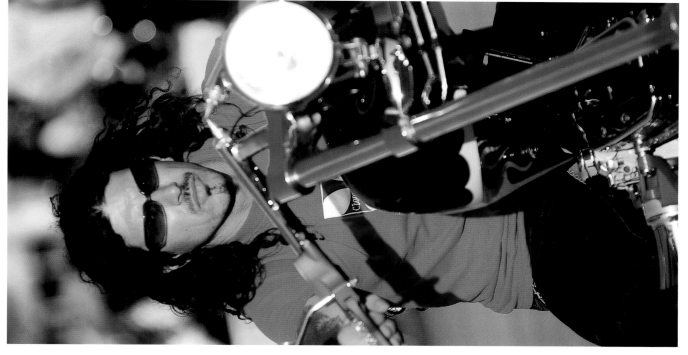

motorcycles that they had seen, or even ridden, overseas. Having lived for years, day in and day out, with their service buddies, a lot of guys also found that hanging out with a bunch of other ex-GIs on motorcycles satisfied their need for "male bonding." Most any combat veteran will tell you that they have never felt closer to any human in their lives than they did to their service buddies. Motorcycles offered a reasonable substitute for adrenaline-charged action, buddy at your side. Some have drawn a comparison between this group of vets that ended up out West, looking to resettle, and the post–Civil War vets that aimlessly drifted out West and became cowboys.

The official Harley ads of the day continued to show tie-clad squares with caps and boots, with the exception of a few that offered pictures of some fellow in a flannel shirt, dungarees, and engineer boots. This may have been a slight nod to the growing underbelly of a very real subculture.

Another factor that influenced the motorcycling scene was the post-war surplus of military Harleys. Hundreds were coming back to the States aboard ships, and any ex-serviceman could buy one for a hundred bucks. Often, the machines that weren't bought were dumped overboard or buried in mass graves.

Many, if not most, of the new owners of these military machines were not interested in preserving them in their orig- inal condition. They stripped off every part that wasn't necessary for function. Smaller gas tanks were fashioned, along with smaller seats, and fenders were chopped off. Thus, the "chopper" was born.

California has long been the birthplace of various subcul- tures: surfing, hot-rodding, Beats, and hippies. It also gave birth to the biker and bikerism. In the mid-forties, groups of the

aforementioned vets started forming cycle clubs. These clubs consisted of guys who got together on the weekends to ride around the countryside, drink some beer, and blow off steam. They wanted to spend time raising a little hell, like drag racing and burnout contests, and drinking with their buddies. The races they conducted weren't sanctioned by the American Motorcycling Association (AMA), and therefore were called outlaw races, thus coining the term "outlaw club."

Many motorcycle clubs that existed before the war were composed of couples and families, usually sanctioned by the AMA. Kids tucked in a sidecar, they would set off for a weekend picnic, and some field games, such as the slow race or the suit- case change, where riders would stop in the middle of the course and change their clothes for the costumes in the case.

Since the birth of the motorcycle, folks had been racing them, and the races often attracted some of these clubs as a des- tination. The AMA was usually the major sponsor of various races. It had been formed in the 1920s, and existed primarily to promote motorcycling as a form of good, clean, all-American fun. It became inevitable that these two disparate groups with opposite outlooks should collide. And they finally did, in a small California town called Hollister.

Hollister was a peaceful farming community of about 4,000 people. It was the major producer of garlic in the United States and the kind of place where "the commander of the local American Legion is by definition a civic leader," as Hunter S. Thompson puts it in his revolutionary book, *Hells Angels*. On Fourth of July 1947, Hollister was hosting a hill climb that had attracted groups from miles around. One of the groups that made the scene was the Booze Fighters, a club that had a simi-

lar reputation to the one eventually possessed by the Hells Angels.

The night before had seen several thousand cyclists drift into town. The local police force of seven men was exhausted and exasperated as they tried to keep the lid on the growing crowd. Drag races were being conducted up and down Main Street. And for the most part, this was the extent of the trouble. The media got hold of the story, even staging a famous photo, and blew the story way out of proportion. This entire incident was depicted in Stanley Kramer's 1953 film, *The Wild One*. The two main characters in this film were diametrically opposed: Johnny, Marlon Brando's character, a disturbed rebel with a heart of gold, and Lee Marvin's character, a just plain mean SOB, who craved power like a sociopath.

Although *The Wild One* was a romanticized Hollywood version of the incident, Thompson calls it "an inspired piece of film journalism, in that it demonstrated a phenomenon that was in its infancy, rather than institutionalizing common knowledge." The motorcycling phenomenon that had come to the press's attention in '47 at Hollister continued to draw fairly small numbers, until the release of *The Wild One*. The film inspired thousands and thousands more to replicate the biker lifestyle. A minute subculture became a part of the cultural lexicon and grew expo-nentially. The film created a more youthful phenomenon, with teenagers and early twentysomethings joining up to rebel against "whatever you got." The image of the motorcycle outlaw became a part of the larger American culture.

Thompson says that the motorcycle outlaw is "as uniquely American as jazz. . . . They were a weird combination of the Wild West cowboy, combined with the great angst of the WWII vet. They reveled in brawling, boozing and transported their ideas of fun in a highly mobile traveling party. They were by definition dangerous hoodlums on big fast motorcycles." Joining up with other groups of cycle gangs, they visited unsuspecting towns of civilians who were totally unprepared for this un-American brand of fun. Thompson further claims that these gangs introduced many of the rural and coastal towns of the period to tourism. They were out, they were about, and put hundreds of miles on their bikes over the course of a normal weekend.

Throughout the fifties, California, and to a lesser degree other areas of the country, continued to spawn outlaw gangs. In San Francisco, a group of cycle hoodlums hung out on Market Street and hence dubbed themselves the Market Street Commandos. Hell-raisers and racers, these guys owned Market Street for a year or two, racing up and down, until a lone stranger rode into town, sporting a death's head on his vest.

Rocky was a Berdoo guy (San Bernardino, California). In a 1964 article, in the *San Francisco Chronicle*, Rocky was described as "a handsome devil, sporting a pointed beard and a derby." The Commandos respected that he could outride the other guys like mad on his chopped, tweaked, extended forked Sportster. He was a Hells Angel from Berdoo.

The Hells Angels' actual origin is lost in time and lore. It is generally thought that the club formed in Fontana, a steel town near Berdoo. The source of the name is also lost to history. It may have been from a bomber squadron with that name, or perhaps the 1930s movie of the same name. Whatever the case, the name caught somebody's imagination and fired up the Berdoo crowd. With the appearance of Rocky, the Angels soon had a second chapter in Frisco, with about forty guys wearing the sinister grinning death's head stitched to vests and jackets.

From that point, the HAs spread out over California. Until the mid-sixties, they were a little-known phenomenon. It was then that they received national attention in a series of articles by *Time, Newsweek*, and other media heavy hitters. The sudden interest was sparked by a series of riots, brawls, and tavern trashings. It seemed as if an evil force had descended upon small-town California. The media accounts often varied wildly from those of eyewitnesses. Soon the Angels inspired panic among civilians that spread to the government, which prepared a massive report known as the Lynch Report, after the California attorney general.

According to the Lynch Report, there were over a thousand roving, drooling, raping pillagers in the state. Actual numbers were probably closer to three or four hundred, tops. The Report made good reading and the press gobbled it up. The Hells Angels were media celebrities and a part of the American cul-tural consciousness.

The HAs soon spread out over the West and even made forays into the East Coast. Other clubs had sprung up back East, with the Pagans representing the largest numbers by the mid-sixties.

Whether it was a small, local club or a regional club, the outlaws had at least two things in common: bikes and philosophy. The "chopped" Harley was the heart of the outlaw world. As most of the bikers at this time were riding the old Knuckleheads or Panheads, the machine itself was huge and heavy, with a rigid frame. The bikers were chopping down the fenders, lengthening and stretching the frames, and tweaking the engines far beyond the realm of the stock bike. Short exhaust pipes with no baffles created a sound and a fury that was meant

to—and did—inspire fear, loathing, and general curiosity wherever they went.

The next big event in biker history was the release of the 1969 film *Easy Rider*. The film inspired a whole new generation to leave suburbia behind, bound for the road astride a Harley-Davidson. A generation who felt the need to divorce themselves from society, yet didn't buy the peace and love crap of the hippies. Many were Vietnam vets, freshly home, confused and full of loathing for the society that had dumped them in a jungle, with no real means to win the war that they and their buddies had died for. The *Easy Rider* image of the biker worked for the outcasts pushed out of society by the culture itself and their own sense of loathing. The new biker became a menacing, dangerous vision of the hippie. Square, middle-class America's worst nightmare had come true.

In the years after *Easy Rider*, the drug scene changed. Hard drugs entered the scene, and in a sense, this was the factor that transitioned the clubs into real outlaws. Many bikers began to traffic and in the process became outright criminals rather than local hell-raisers.

By the eighties most clubs were being vigorously pursued by the feds on drug charges, bolstered by the RICO Act, used to gut the Mafia and other branches of organized crime. This view by law enforcement, that all bikers were drug dealers and members of organized crime, had a huge ripple effect on the Harley rider in general.

Most Harley fanatics, under the age of forty or so, were or saw themselves as some variation on the hardcore gang member. The romance of the characters in *The Wild One* and *Easy Rider* had a wide appeal to many who were not interested in

gang activity, yet shared the same basic need for the Harley, the biker philosophy, and a general loathing of middle-class values.

The heart of the biker philosophy was the Harley. No other brand could or would be considered, except maybe an old Indian. Stock motorcycles became customized personal statements, a flag in the face of society.

The soul of the biker philosophy was brotherhood. Bikers put complete faith in their brothers. A "righteous biker" would rather perish than not back up a brother. Right or wrong, the stance of your brothers had to be your own. Society sucked, and in most cases, had cast the biker aside years before he ever straddled a bike. Society's rules did not apply, because they were meant to keep the squares square. One never lied to a brother. Bikers believed in complete honesty among themselves. Outsiders were not subject to the same rules, and therefore had few rights.

Bikers mainly wanted to be left alone. In most cases, when a fracas occurred, it was sparked by an outsider, by an act of aggression or a sign of disrespect. Bikers have always been big on respect among themselves, and tolerate no disrespect from outsiders or insiders who disregard designated lines. Retaliation is often massive and immediate, among brothers and against squares. Bikers have a huge capacity for respect of authority, but an authority chosen, not imposed.

The exploitive films of the sixties and seventies created an image of a mindless animal dedicated to violence and anarchy. Bikers laughed at these films, knowing that they lived by a stricter code than most squares. It was their lust for living for today, with little thought for or belief in the future that scared the squares. A true biker would go much farther, faster, to prove their point than most any square.

Put into a narrow frame, the biker philosophy was that of the fatalist. No helmets, 'cause he'd rather die anyway rather than get screwed up and live like a vegetable. Spend every dime today, 'cause tomorrow might not come. What some might regard as a lack of respect for life, the biker sees as a giant love of life and living.

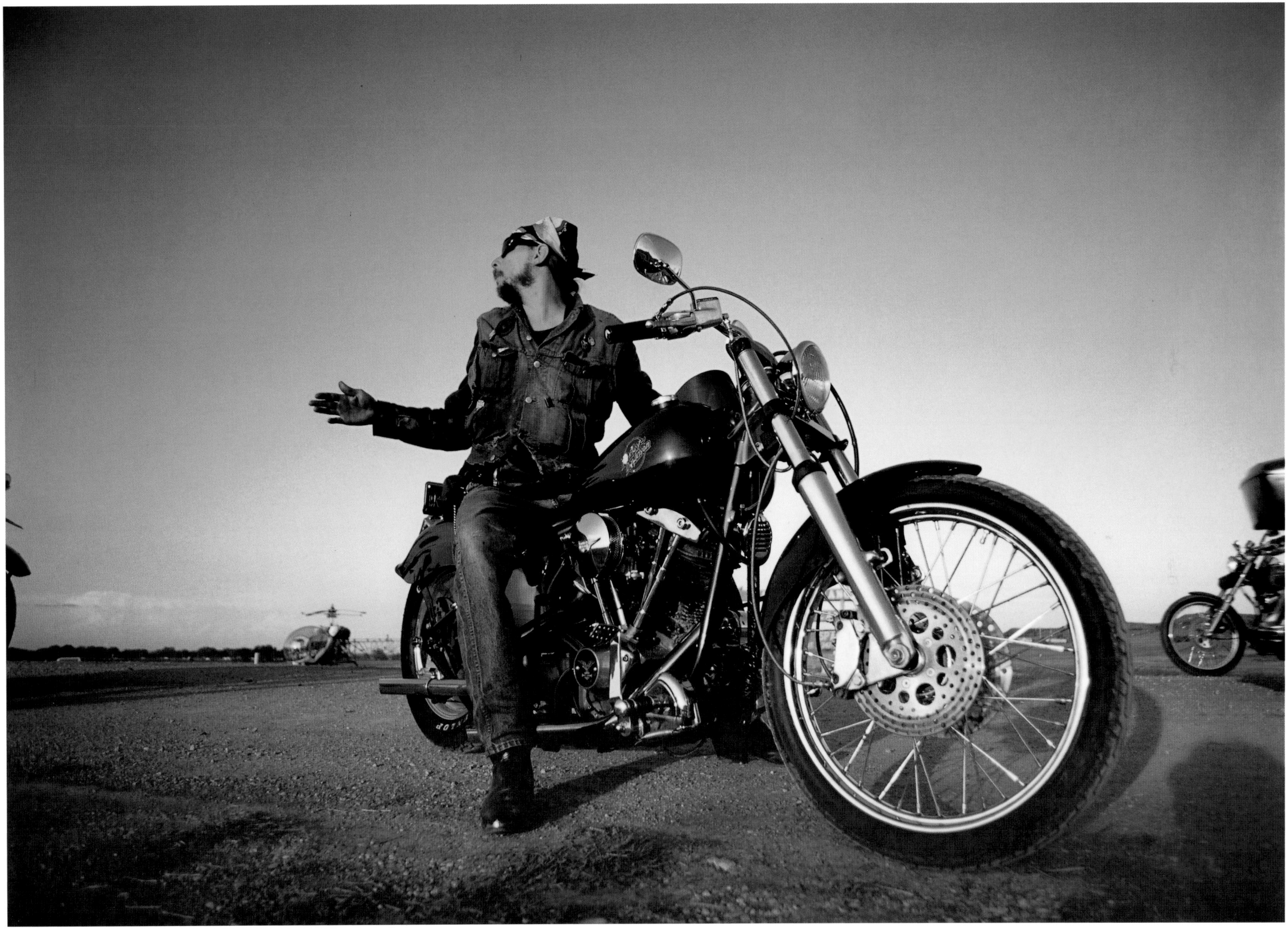

SHOVELHEAD, STURGIS, 1984

CHAPTER FOUR:

The racers of the day were a breed apart. In fact, they were in many ways gypsies themselves. They lived by a code of what Sturgis historian Carl Edeburn called "mutual sharing and support." None of these early racers made any real money. They all worked winter jobs and barely scraped by during the season. They were their own mechanics, yet often competitors would lend a hand, a wrench, or parts to each other.

Sturgis, South Dakota, is a small town snuggled into the Black Hills. With a population of 6,500, it is similar to thousands of small towns throughout the West. It developed as an agricultural center, which had the dual purpose of servicing the Fort Meade cavalry post, established in 1878. Sturgis served as the gateway to the Deadwood gold mines. In its early days it was populated by ranchers, farmers, soldiers, and camp followers, as well as merchants and the general population it takes to run a town. Its history, like its appearance, is no different than many other Western towns. So how is it that this obscure town became the mecca of motorcycle rallies?

In order for the Black Hills Motorcycle Classic to come into being, it took a combination of forces, one of which came in the form of a fellow by the name of Clarence "Pappy" Hoel. Pappy Hoel was the son of a part-time freighter, cattleman, and ice dealer. He was born in Sturgis and spent his whole life there. As a young man, he became enamored with motorcycles and came to own several Indians while he was still fairly young. He was a product of the West, independent, tough, with an unwavering dedication to his ideals. He loved tradition, yet dealt with a world that was changing all around him. He respected the individual, and expected the same in return. Pappy took no crap.

He inherited the ice business from his father, yet saw that the advent of electric refrigeration was going to put an end to his enterprise. With the Great Depression coming down on top of him at the same time, he looked for another opportunity. With the blessing of his young—and apparently brave—new bride, Pearl, he decided to get into the motorcycle repair and sales business. Although he was an Indian enthusiast, he

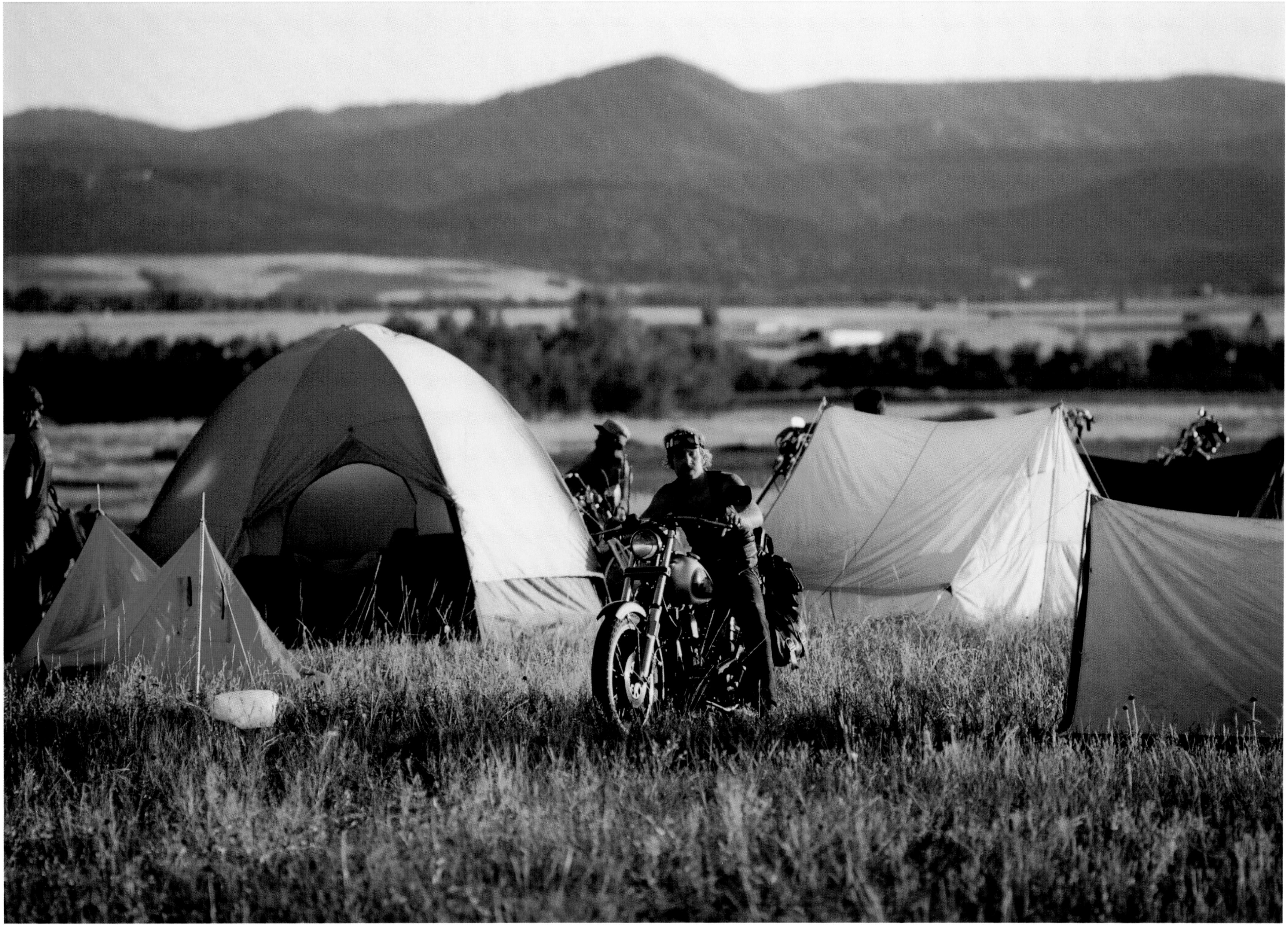

CAMPING AT THE BUFFALO CHIP, STURGIS, 1984

approached Harley for a dealership and was turned down. He next approached Indian, and despite having no financial backing, only a dream in hand, was granted a dealership. In order to have a brand-new bike to use as a demonstrator, he sold a friend a bike at cost, with the understanding that he would use it to demo for potential buyers.

By 1936, he was successful enough that he was able to build a new house with a large garage, which was to serve as his shop and dealership. A place for the local boys to hang out, swapping stories and telling lies.

Many of the local boys switched over to Indians from Harley in order to support Pappy, and also to avoid making the 35-mile trip to Rapid City for parts. Out of his own enthusiasm for motorcycles, and also due to his shrewd promotional sense, Pappy was soon heading up a club of local riders. They would get together for picnics, field trials, and midnight runs, often taking along their wives and girlfriends. One day, while on a run, the club stopped for a picnic. A man in a car came along and called out, "You know what you fellows look like?" "No," came the reply, and the man responded with, "A bunch of gypsies." And so the Jackpine Gypsies Motorcycle Club was born.

Though they formed a club in 1936, they received official AMA sanctioning in '37. Pappy had been a member for a couple of years and wanted the club to have official sanctioning. The club had 18 original members, and was to become another force in the creation of the world's largest motorcycle event, known the world over as "Sturgis."

The club met weekly to collect dues and discuss business, which might consist of a four-week-long discussion of how much to spend on a new coffee pot, and always included the

nickel raffle, where everybody put in a nickel, and the winner grossed 90 cents. The club often got together with the Rapid City Pioneer Motorcycle Club (RPMs) for their rides, picnics, and field meets. In 1937 they decided to rejuvenate the old half-mile horse racing track at the Meade County fairgrounds. Club members weeded the old track and had it graded. Once the hard work was done, it was time to play hard.

Innocent of how momentous the decision was to become, the Jack Pine boys decided to host a meet at their new track. Naturally it was Pappy who instigated, planned, and managed the event. He seemed to have a knack for having one eye on a good time and one on promoting his Indian dealership, and motorcycling in general. The Gypsies invited the RPMs and the club from Lead. They were to do a few stunts, some of the field events, and have a race. About nine of the club members raced that day, but apparently the general attendance was quite large. Several members of the Sturgis business community took notice.

In 1938, several members of the Sturgis "Commercial Club," a branch of the Chamber of Commerce, began stumping for an official rally to be managed not by the Gypsies or the RPMs, but the town's business and community leaders. The realization that this event could be used to generate revenue was clearly a unique opportunity for a town without a lot of major industry. Merchants would benefit, and any money raised would go to charity. In a display of social consciousness, perhaps too in step with the times, the Commercial Club didn't want to include any of the Gypsies unless they were also business owners. Thus, Pappy and a couple of the other Gypsies were allowed to become members of the actual committee that was set up to oversee the event. The committee formed a corporation known

as the Black Hills Motor Classic (BHMC). The Commercial Club committee enlisted the help of the Sturgis City Council, the Gypsies and the RPMs. By including the RPMs as volunteers, they hoped to bring in more people from the neighboring town of Rapid City.

They planned a parade with bikes, business floats, a Gypsy tour, races, stunts, and field events. Pappy, in his usual shrewd manner, did two very clever things. He applied to the AMA to make the races a sanctioned event, and sold $2 memberships to the businessmen of the community. The Gypsy tour was an AMA term for a group ride, not a reference to the club's name. Although turned away by the Commercial Club, the actual running of the events fell on the Jackpine Gypsies Club members and the RPMs. Seven hundred fifty dollars was raised in prize money and nine riders from eight states signed up. Pappy did his famous burning wall crash, were he crashed through a flam-

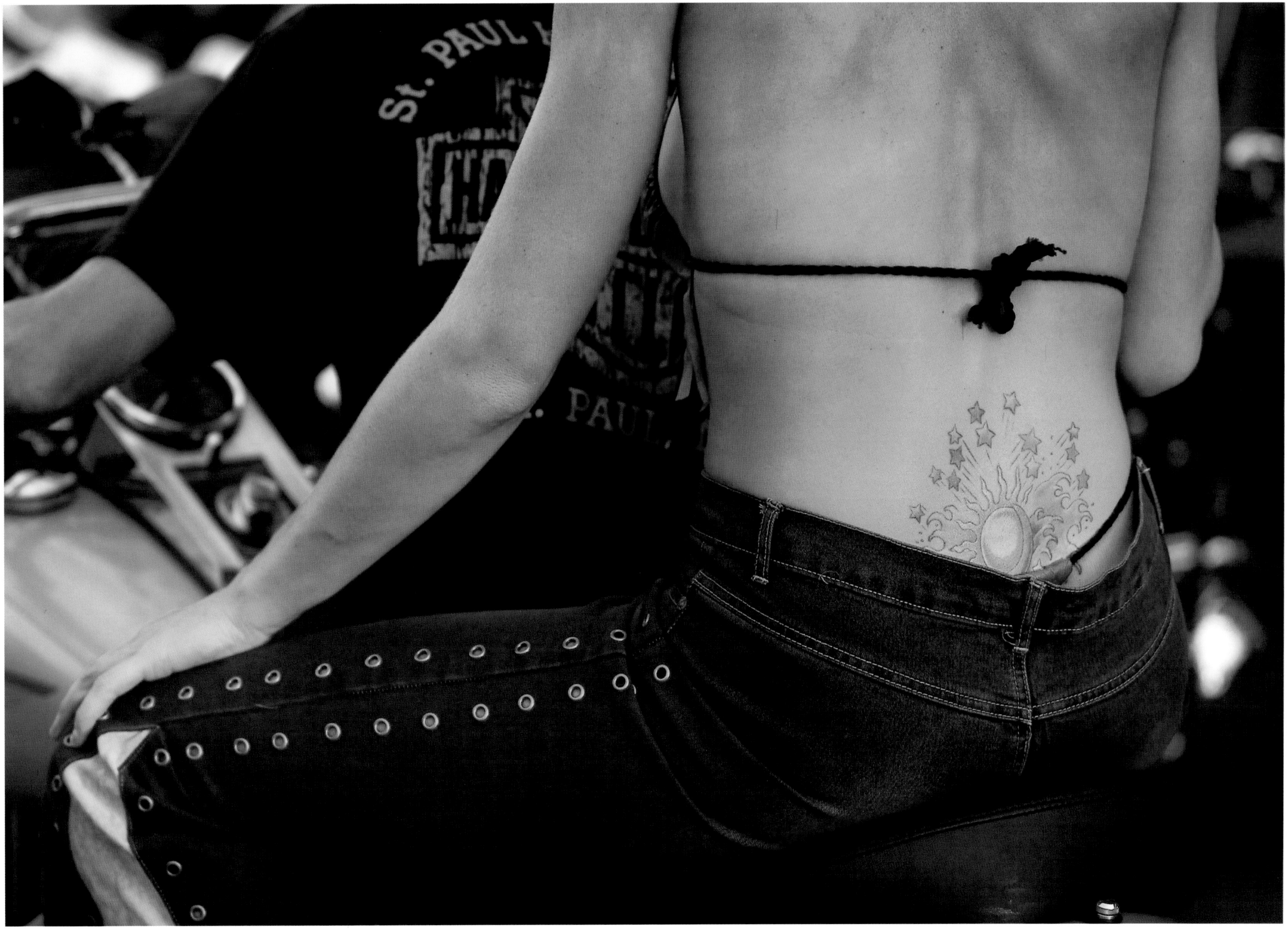

SUNBURST, MAIN STREET, STURGIS, 2002

PUBLIC PARKING, DEADWOOD, SOUTH DAKOTA, 2003

ing wall made of sticks. Seven Indians and two Harleys competed in the official race and also held challenge pairs to extend the entertainment. Thus the Black Hills Motor Classic—the Sturgis rally of today—was created.

In the following years, before the war, the BHMC continued to expand. Pappy continued as the chief manager and organizer and was always at the head of the pack during the Gypsy tour. The format for the tour remained the same for many years. The riders would leave Sturgis, head to Mt. Rushmore, the Needles Highway, the state game lodge, and by Sylvan Lake. At the halfway point, Pearl Hoel and one or two of her girlfriends would have a lunch cooked and ready for the riders. Wieners, potato salad, beans, and iced tea or coffee—all for sixty-five cents a person. She would follow the pack back to Sturgis, providing a support vehicle for any breakdowns. Upon their return to Sturgis, the riders would meet up at the City Park for a dinner feed, some clean-cut entertainment, and prizes for the best-dressed, oldest, youngest, and longest distance traveled to Sturgis.

By 1941, the event had grown to include a couple of thousand spectators, one hundred riders on the tour, and thirty racers, all drawn from many states both east and west. However, war seemed inevitable and in '41 a patriotic ceremony was added to the venue. This was in fact the last BHMC until 1946.

Immediately after the war, in 1946, and in the years following the restarting of the rally, the event continued to grow. Pappy's dealership continued to prosper, partially because of the boom times, but largely through the force of his personality, and his extremely kind and caring nature. There are many stories concerning Pappy's generosity. He always made sure that the racers had enough money to move onto their next stop. He gave

them gas money or even food when necessary. As a consequence, the BHMC earned a fine reputation among racers.

The racers of the day were a breed apart. In fact, they were in many ways gypsies themselves. They lived by a code of what Sturgis historian Carl Edeburn called "mutual sharing and support." None of these early racers made any real money. They all worked winter jobs and barely scraped by during the season. They were their own mechanics, yet often competitors would lend a hand, a wrench, or parts to each other. They slept in their cars, a haystack, or even scammed a motel room for a couple of hours after the guest had checked out. They did all of this for the thrill of racing and the comradeship they shared on the road.

During the fifties the rally continued to grow with about 6,000 spectators and sixty or more racers. The event was getting national press from the motorcycle magazines, which no doubt fueled its growth. The BHMC was the site for several Five-Mile National Championship Races in the early fifties which increased the popularity of the rally for the racers. The racing field was no longer filled with only American bikes; more and more British bikes were racing and doing well.

In the first years of the rally, most of the attendees camped in the Hoels' yard under a large tent that the couple rented each year. When there was no more space under the tent, the yard and shop filled up. In the morning, the Hoels would serve coffee and doughnuts which sustained the riders until lunch on the days when there was a tour. As crowds grew, the City Park began to fill up with campers of all ages. It continued to be the site of the Friday-night feed where buffalo was generally the main course. There were quite a few female riders even in those early days, some riding from as far as Ohio and even Florida.

Women started to make the scene with the Motor Maids, a club solely for female riders that was chartered in 1940. It received AMA sanctioning the following year with a membership of over fifty women. The Maids were often seen at charity and motorcycle events, riding in formation with their white gloves on. In those days they were welcomed as a novelty, but many of the club members were just as deadly serious about their riding as the men.

The rally received widespread support throughout its early decades. The local newspaper often published articles and editorial pieces publicizing the event and they promoting the riders who attended as responsible citizens. They were not "scatterbrained," and they were members of the AMA, a highly respectable organization, dedicated to wiping out the "outlaw" faction who were scofflaws and ignored the rules concerning safety and noise. It was and always had been a family event. It was not unusual to see two or even three kids in a sidecar, with mom and dad on the inadequate seats of the old Harleys and Indians. If there was any drinking it was well concealed, and even the dance was a tame family event.

Community support of the rally was in fact expanding during the fifties, with more and more local organizations getting involved in rally support, and benefiting financially from the activity. The newspapers were quick to point out that rally proceeds from the BHMC committee went to benefit such groups as the Boy Scouts, school band, the community pool, and the local fire department.

The rally continued to grow at a steady rate as the sixties wound on. Apparently, in 1965, there was a scare that the Hells Angels were going to show up and take over the town. There was no demonstrable fact for the scare, and seems to be a result of rumor, rather than any fact. This was the year that the Lynch Report had been published and the HAs had received a huge amount of publicity through the national news. The sheriff reassured the town that local law enforcement had things well in hand, and reminded everyone that the vast majority of motorcyclists were "merely normal people who have a fondness for riding free as the wind, and not beatniks as some people believe." Families and the Gypsies were still well in control of the event.

Despite the social upheaval evident elsewhere in the country, the people of Sturgis managed to stay relatively isolated from the massive changes sweeping the country in the sixties. Local boys had volunteered and been drafted to Vietnam, but for the most part long hair, beads, sandals, and drugs had remained unknown in Sturgis. And there were no demonstrations against the war taking place in the streets. But one of the unintended side effects of the rally was that it brought popular American culture to Sturgis, if only for a week.

The late sixties brought signs of the changing youth culture rolling in to town, and along with it the first real signs of trouble to the rally. In '68 some rowdy behavior occurred at the City Park after the feed and entertainment program. No record of any specifics is left behind, but it can be surmised that it was the result of youngsters overindulging in too much booze. There are few facts available that give any further specifics of "the trouble." It would seem that in the process of becoming lore, many of the facts were exaggerated over the years, and any incidents of trouble have become wildly exaggerated, the result of bad reputation, fertile imaginations, and mostly media hype.

Another incident occurred when a small group of bikers lit gasoline across the road between Sturgis and Ft. Meade, daring motorcyclists to pass through it. Most did it without hesitation (the alternative being to stop next to a pack of wild-looking bikers), but the police were quickly on hand to shut it down. By the next year, officials were planning to increase the presence of law enforcement by including military air police from nearby Ellsworth Airforce Base.

Then Sheriff Eggers referred to the troublemakers as "hippie-type cyclists" and pointed out that they made up a minute portion of those in attendance. He blamed the trouble on a group of about twenty "hippie types," who rode machines that were in clear violation of South Dakota State Motor Vehicle Code (read: loud choppers) and who refused to wear helmets, as was required at the time. The '69 rally passed without incidence, and the mayor praised the conduct of the motorcyclists, and further noted that many had applauded the atmosphere of law and order. The ability of town officials to anticipate and plan for growth and contingencies became a hallmark of those in charge.

This flexibility is probably due to the realization of the economic impact that the rally had on the town and the surrounding area. It was estimated that at $30 per day, with a minimum attendance of three days per person, each 1,000 visitors were leaving behind $100,000—this, in an area that had no real industry to speak of, other than farming and ranching. The town officials and the business community were going to protect the rally, no matter what it took.

In 1971, Sturgis was making the national news. Roger Mudd and a CBS crew were on hand to tape some of the bikes

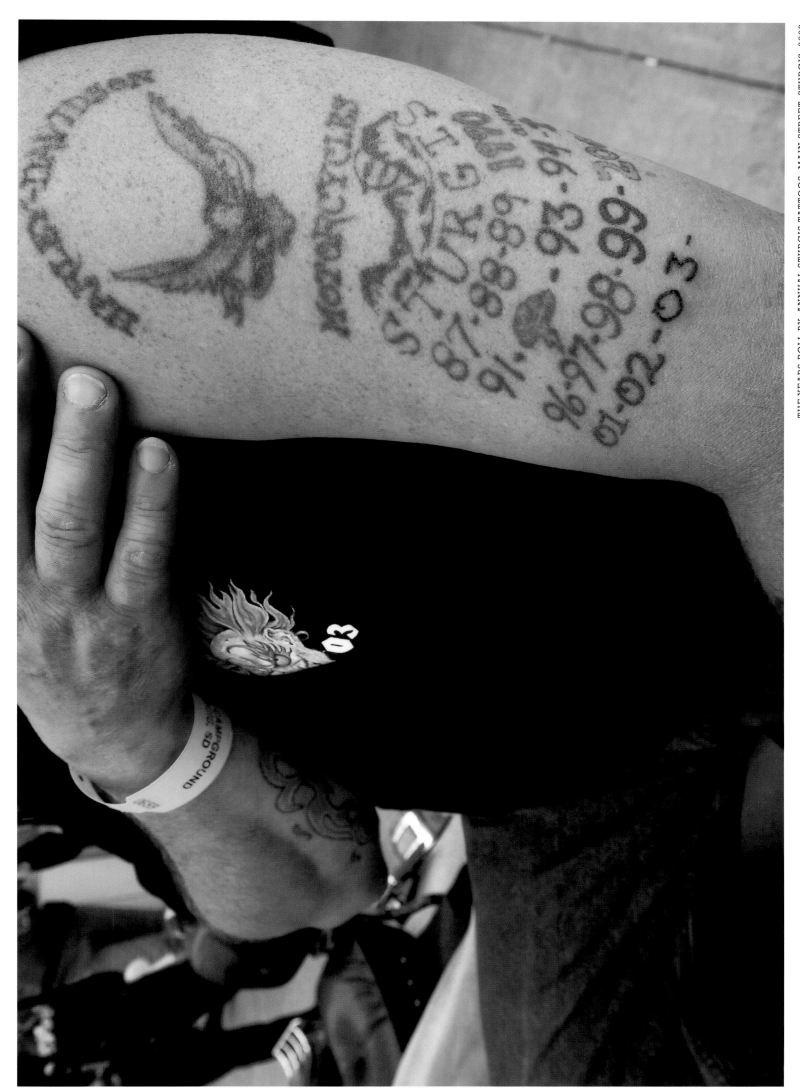

setting out on the Gypsy tour. The five-minute segment included an overhead shot of the tour from a helicopter. By this time the number of motorcyclist publications had grown, and the younger, biker-type reader had their own publication, *Easyriders* magazine.

The magazine was dedicated to showing the best in custom rides and portraying the biker lifestyle. It is through publicity in the magazine that younger riders received news of the rally in the Black Hills. It seemed like a great place to party.

By the mid-seventies, attendance was reaching the 18,000 mark, a far cry from a couple of thousand in the early days. The rally was extended to a seven-day format, with the Gypsy tour taking place in what amounted to shifts. This new format for the tour had come about when the line of bikes stretched for a solid eight miles. The focus for most riders continued to center around the races and the tour.

By 1976, attendance at the rally surpassed 18,000. By Monday, City Park and Boulder Canyon campgrounds were filled to capacity, and some riders had taken to pitching tents along the interstate, outside of town. Later in the week, trouble arose in City Park. A lot of beer was consumed and territorial squabbles broke out as the park was packed to capacity. Ignoring the presence of many families, people were taking their clothes off and parading around the place. At one point on Friday night someone set up a backlit screen and various couples put on a sexual version of shadow puppets. Once again a group of riders lit a strip across the road between Ft. Meade and Sturgis and dared riders to pass through. Most of the cyclists proceeded without hesitation, but some automobile drivers refused, creating a traffic snarl. Police quickly shut down both situations, but the reaction in the aftermath was nothing short of furious.

The experience of 1976 made it evident that there was an undercurrent of dislike for the rally by many of the local residents. Most of the complaints seemed irrational and centered around self-serving viewpoints. But there was no way that the powers that be were going to put an end to the one great financial boon the area had.

In order to deal with the problems at City Park, a unique arrangement was reached. A local businessman, Eddie Lawson, agreed to lease the park and therefore became responsible for the security and behavior of the campers. Lawson divided the park into two sections and reserved one area for families and elderly people. This arrangement suited most parties and stayed in place until 1982, when camping in the park ended forever. Despite Lawson's best attempts, the lascivious behavior combined with such freelance events as burnout contests continued, and the residents of Sturgis revolted against the wildness. Those that enjoyed the wild times in the park still reminisce about what a real party it was.

Although law enforcement characterized the next few years as quite subdued, a growing element of the public disliked the larger crowds, and the import of the permissive American culture, or more accurately, subculture. Editorials in the local press made a hard turn and were not as supportive as they had been in previous years. One editor wrote that the "strangers" were "wiping their feet on the carpet" of the locals' values.

There was also a growing resentment against those who were making money off of the rally from those who weren't reaping the benefits. Receipts for camping at City Park had doubled between '78 and '79. The local merchants were obviously benefiting and a core of entrepreneurs were getting a nice take from the rally. Some of those opposed to the rally may have been ignoring the amount of the proceeds that went to the local charities or were made by many church groups that served up breakfast.

City officials continued to seek solutions to the problems caused by the growing pains. The chief of police sent out letters to all the law enforcement agencies in the state inviting the officers to come work at the rally and assuring them he would pay their wages. This unique solution was effective and remains in place today.

The eighties marked a real change in the BHMC. The races started to take a backseat as the main form of entertainment. More and more visitors weren't even attending the Gypsy tour; they were touring around the area by themselves or in small groups. More and more people came for the social scene. Although characterized by some as the "gang years," the vast majority of attendees were not even close to being members of outlaw gangs. Many riders did seek group affiliation, and found

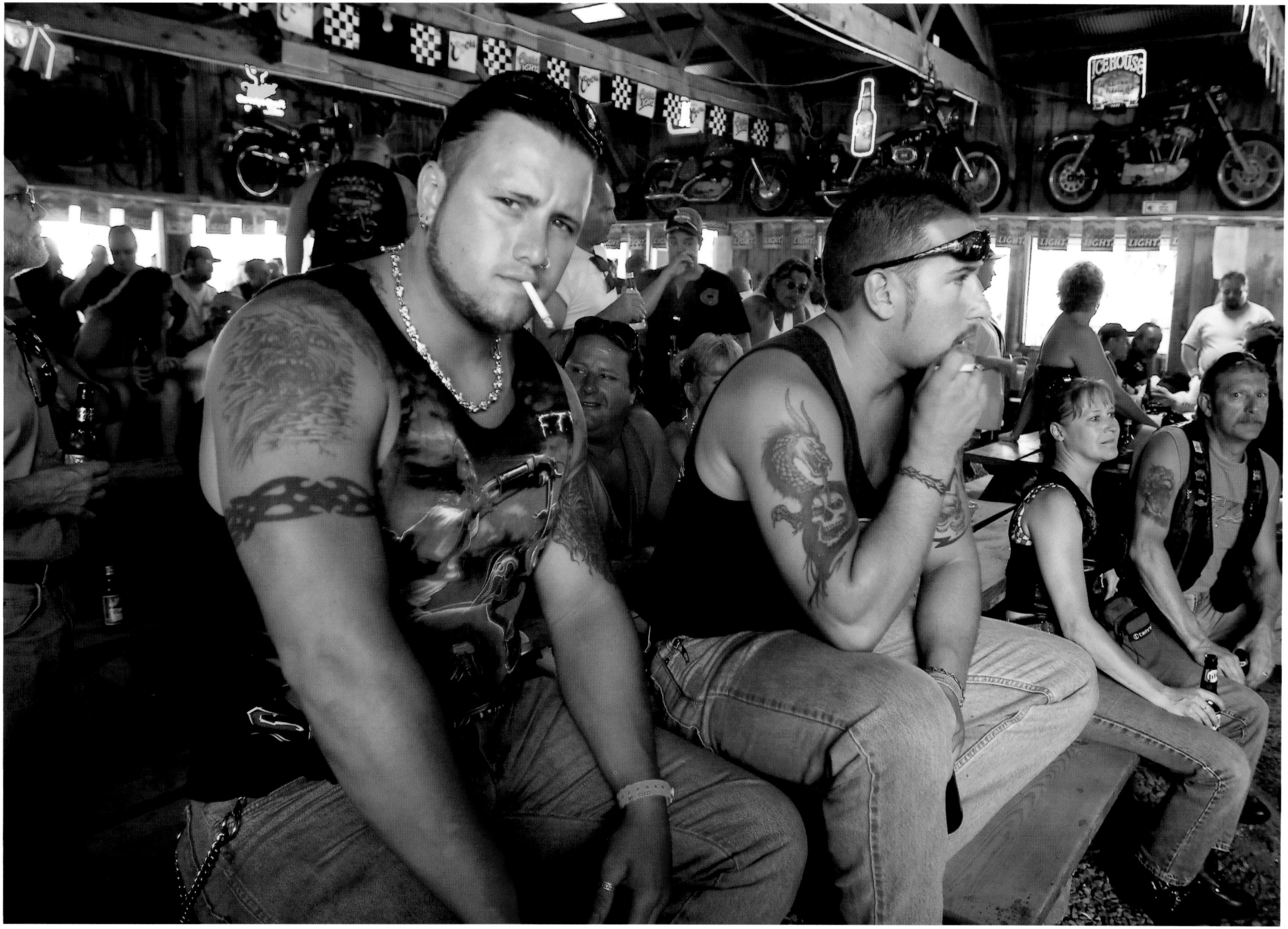

BROKEN SPOKE, STURGIS, 2002

it in such organizations as the Christian Motorcyclist Association or in the factory-sponsored group HOG. And motorcycling itself began to change. In 1982, Harley began selling the Evolution motor. For the first time in the company's history they had a motor that was reliable and oil-drip free. The new reliability of Harleys attracted a whole new type of motorcyclist. Many riders who had been riding European or Japanese bikes for their reliability started buying Harleys. It seemed that there was a huge contingent of motorcyclists who had wanted them all along. One effect of the new reliable engines was that the Harley was no longer the domain of the working class. As a generalization, the working class are more comfortable working with their hands, as many use them for a living. When Harleys no longer required traveling with a tool kit, more and more middle- and upper-middle-class buyers became interested.

Many celebrities, such as Mickey Rourke and Tommy Lee, were now seen on the new Harleys, and this added to the general attraction. The average Harley rider was more educated, financially better off, older, and of course better behaved. These factors contributed to the rally staying alive even as attendance skyrocketed.

The man who started it all, Pappy Hoel, and his wife, Pearl, saw forty-nine rallies together. Without his dedication, foresight, wisdom, and the mighty support of Pearl, it is doubtful the rally would have continued for so many years. Pappy wanted to see the fiftieth anniversary, which fell in 1990. He didn't quite make it; he died in February of that year, just a few months shy. When asked, Pearl says she believes that he would be pleased to see what the rally evolved into over the years. His tireless promotion of motorcycling and his hometown created the largest rally in the world. And if pressed, this modest man might even express some pride in his life's work.

The fiftieth anniversary of Sturgis attracted a record-breaking 350,000 people. At the time, a crowd that large was almost inconceivable. And it went off without a hitch. It was well-organized and well-enforced. The crowds declined slightly for a number of years afterwards, and then started to rise again.

In the nineties the flavor of the rally began to change again. A professional event manager—instead of the old, BHMC committee, which was derived from the Commercial Club—managed the event. When the event became too large to handle in the eighties, the BHMC had handed control over to the city council, which soon tired of the job and, probably wisely, handed control over to the professionals.

Another factor that changed the flavor of the rally was the decision to return it to a family-type event, as was originally intended. It soon became evident that the switch was successful, as the crowds became more and more family-oriented, and therefore more subdued.

The year 2000 saw the sixtieth anniversary come and go. This time the crowd was reported to consist of over 600,000 people. Once again, the event was well-managed and an unbelievable success.

Over the years Sturgis has become more and more a commercial event. Vendors of every possible description are everywhere, and their numbers continue to multiply. The price for space has steadily increased, and some of the vendors simply bought up the property along Main Street, with many of the old locals making a tidy profit as a benefit from climbing real estate values. Other real estate investors have bought up houses and rent them out during the rally at prices that apparently cover the mortgage.

The races have almost completely taken a backseat to other activities at the rally. Many of the new visitors are completely unaware of the existence of the races. In the eighties drag racing was introduced at Belle Fouche and they have been a big draw. The Gypsies still have their short track, moto-cross, and hillclimb courses, and are in no danger of going away.

The miracle of the BHMC is that it has continued to grow and at the same time thrive as the people in charge have anticipated and adjusted to the changes required by the ever-increasing crowds. Perhaps the real miracle is that it has survived these increasingly litigious times. It is a credit to the people of Sturgis that the event continues to exist, and the residents for the most part are happy to have over 500,000 people take over their town. Perhaps it is the Western ideals of community that have kept it going; where the squeaky wheel doesn't get the grease, the good of the majority is the rule. But it is undeniable that credit is largely due to Pappy and, in later years, the spirit of that tough, kind, and gutsy man.

The racers of the day were a breed apart. In fact, they were in many ways gypsies themselves. They lived by a code of what Sturgis historian Carl Edeburn called "mutual sharing and support." None of these early racers made any real money. They all worked winter jobs and barely scraped by during the season. They were their own mechanics, yet often competitors would lend a hand, a wrench, or parts to each other.

As I come over the hill by the Ellsworth Airforce Base, the Black Hills come into view. They rise magnificently out of the surrounding prairie, and are indeed black when viewed at a distance, due to their coverage of pine trees. Ellsworth is just a short hop to Rapid City, which is thirty-five miles from Sturgis. At one time Rapid just occupied a valley, but like all thriving towns, has expanded and is rapidly climbing the surrounding hills. I even notice some subdivisions that are forming a small-town version of suburbia. As I pass by Rapid City, I remember reading that in many ways Pappy was able to get the whole ball rolling with the help of the Rapid City Pioneer Motorcycle Club, and because of the competition between them and the Jack Pine Gypsies.

Every mile closer to Sturgis, I see the number of motorcycles increase. They swarm around the cars and due to sheer numbers seem to dwarf the automobiles. As I have done over the years, I pass Exit 30, which leads into the south end of town, and proceed to Exit 32 on the north side. I always feel like I get into the action faster this way, as I don't have to pass through the older residential district to get to the center of town. This route also brings me by the Jackpine Gypsies track, and I indulge in a moment where I imagine all the vintage bikes buzzing around the track. I count my blessings when I see that the line of bikes on the off ramp is only a hundred yards long or so. There are more people here now, but I can't help that rising sense of excitement and anticipation I get as I proceed into town.

I am quickly engulfed in the proceedings as I slide onto Independence Avenue, which eventually parallels Main Street. Every vendor imaginable, or unimaginable if it is your first time,

PUTTIN' PAST BOB'S, MAIN STREET, STURGIS, 1984

is present on the ride down Independence. I notice that not only are there more vendors in general, but there are also more companies like Iron Horse, which are custom bike builders, allowing anybody with enough money to own a supreme custom machine.

Your senses are overwhelmed the first time you enter the town. You are surrounded by a constant stream of bikes going in both directions, and vendor after vendor doing their thing. I make my way down Main Street and find a place to park behind the auditorium. Parking is usually only a minor problem, but it is wise to keep some singles in your pocket in case you have to pay. It is only a minor expense and you have the security of knowing that your bike is being watched.

I walk over to Independence and cross the street, surrounded by pedestrians of all descriptions. The amount of foot traffic is unbelievable, more like what you would expect in a large city, rather than a town of 6,500. Crushes of the black-and-leather-clad, looking for excitement, new parts, or a really good party.

The noise is incredible. Thousands upon thousands of Harleys and every other bike imaginable sound off at the same time. Surround Sound at high decibels. Not even a racetrack produces this kind of sound. As a bike lover, it's like coming home.

My nephew made me promise to bring him home a studded leather belt. Funny, I guess they are in fashion again with the kids. Haven't had one myself for a long time. I duck into a vendor's tent to get the purchase out of the way. I start talking to one of the salesmen. He's from North Carolina, a computer guy. He helps me out at some of the major events. He finds me the right belt and I deal him down a few bucks. Negotiating at these events can save you a lot of money over the course of your visit. And the vendors don't seem to mind; I think they kind of enjoy it.

Having taken care of my main responsibility, I walk over to Main Street. I remember the first time I hit Main Street, I was with a pack of friends. Lost in the crowd, we made a left turn, and bam, with a sense of shock I realized that I was on the infamous Main Street. Bikes stacked up on either side and back-to-back down the middle. Flashing chrome and glistening paint. I tried to figure out how many bikes I was looking at, but it was like trying to count grains of sand in your hand. You simply lose track and become overwhelmed.

I stand on the corner for a moment and just take it in. People of all shapes and sizes. The crowd is definitely different than years ago. Less hardcore types and more enthusiasts. For years there has been an ongoing argument about who is a "real" biker. The argument can get intense, so I use the all-encompassing term "enthusiasts." Making that kind of judgment—who is "real"— can only be made accurately when you get to know the person, not by looking at them.

I feel the need for a cold one and duck into a tent that is serving as a temporary bar. Beer in hand, I relax, enjoying a little space and a slight reprieve from the noise. About the time I am ready to split, a guy and a lady with HOG insignia on their vests settle in beside me at the bar. They look like old-school bikers, and there is a spark of recognition as we greet each other. They look like old-school Sturgis. The guy has a long beard and an even longer ponytail. The gal wears no makeup, and neither one of them shows any signs of wearing any of the brand name gear that seems so prevalent these days. His name is Murray and her name is Sue, and it turns out that they are from New Zealand. Curiosity piqued, I interrogate them.

They are with a group of thirty-five. They had their bikes shipped over and are on a tour of the States, with Sturgis being one of the major destinations. It is their first time here and I can see that their minds are blown. They just keep grinning as they describe their plans. They met their bikes in L.A. and came up through Nevada, Utah, and Colorado. Murray claims that there are about a total of four hundred HOG members from New Zealand and about eight hundred from Australia who are coming to Sturgis. Their group is going to travel on to New York and then head down through the southern states, back to L.A. We talk briefly about how to tune a bike for that kind of heat, and the best grade of oil to use. They are staying at the Buffalo Chip campground, and invite me out to party with them that evening. There is no way that I am going to turn down a chance to hang at the Buffalo Chip, so I tell them that I will meet them out there after I find something to eat.

WET T-SHIRT CONTEST, WYOMING WEDNESDAY, SUNDANCE, WYOMING, 2002

I drift down Main Street a little farther and check out the food. Gyros seem to be a big item, though I don't remember them from years past. Another place offers huge sausages with onions and peppers stuffed into a bun. Used to be that all a person could find was chili and buffalo burgers. Now there is all kinds of fare to choose from. I settle on an Indian Taco, a mix of ground beef and spices with lettuce, onions, tomatoes, and some hot sauce. The damn thing is huge and I settle down onto a curb to wrestle it and watch the folks go by.

Since I am on the north end of Main Street, I walk over to the photo tower. I have done this for years. I suppose it is twenty feet high or so, and gives you a view of the entire length of Main. I lay down the fee, and snap a shot for the nephew, fulfilling another promise.

I walk most of the length of Main, looking for the new museum. On the way I weave through the crowd, which affords me a look at the merchandise and the people. There has definitely been a demographic change. People are older, and there is a much broader spectrum. There seems to be less evidence of intoxication, and none of the air of impending danger I remember from twenty years ago. All in all I would say it feels more comfortable, but that may be a function of my age.

I get down to the south end of Main and find the museum. It is right about where all the outlaw clubs used to hang. I see a few of patch holders, but very few. I duck into the museum, and am excited by the variety of classic bikes. Downstairs there is a Jackpine Gypsies display and other displays honoring the racers. I am immediately intrigued by the display of female riders, the old-timers—especially the story of Dorothy Goulding-Robinson. Dorothy was a pioneer of early motorcycling and enduro racing.

She started riding at age sixteen, in 1928. She was a competitor in two-day and 500-mile events, traveling on sand roads and crossing rivers. In 1935 she did a coast-to-coast run, in 89 hours and 58 minutes. She died at age eighty-seven in 1999. In her lifetime she covered fifteen million miles.

I feel dwarfed in the "presence" of this woman. Her mileage totals makes me feel sheepish at having boasted about my half-mill over the years. That is the thing about thinking you are bad—there is always someone out there who is badder.

I stroll back to the north end and I head out of town on Highway 34, past the old cavalry fort. I have never been, but they have a museum there showing how things were back in the old days. Pappy spent a couple of years there, on and off during WWII maintaining the Harleys and Indians for the troopers. After I've gone about three miles outside of town, I come to the Buffalo Chip campground. The Chip is a Sturgis legend to be sure. The Hells Angels own it. I don't know how that arrangement works, but they bought it in order to have a place to party and not get hassled. They have their own area; the rest is open to the public. I don't know if this is still the arrangement, but they used to have three sections: family, radical, and zoo. Buddha and I stayed in the zoo section one year, and moved to radical on our next visit. We couldn't handle the continuous partying; it never seemed to cease. Had to have somewhere to hole up and rest.

I have a favorite memory of a stay there. I had gotten up and gone for a cup of coffee. I wound my way back through the tents; I saw our friend Chuck had backed his bike up to the tent, which still contained Buddha. Chuck started the bike up and cranked up the revs. He let go of the clutch, throwing a huge

stream of dirt in through the open flaps. After a half-minute or so, he shut it down. Giggling away, we looked in at Buddha. He was sitting there in the lotus position, undisturbed and meditating, with a pile of dirt on his head.

I circle around a little, looking for the Kiwis. The Chip is a real freak show. I see a nude couple riding casually through, and every sort of bizarre costume imaginable. I think this is where all the really outlandish people you see in town stay. I find the Kiwis by locating their New Zealand flag.

I had partied with some Australians over the years and knew them to be some of the craziest drinkers on Earth. Well, the Kiwis at least matched the Aussies. I know at one point we wandered over to see a band at the main stage—I think it was Alice Cooper—and the next thing I know, it is early morning and I am lying half-dressed under a picnic table. I think I'm gonna die of thirst. Seeing no water around, I dump the flowers

out of the vase on the table, and suck the thing dry. I figure that hanging around will just make things more painful, so I start up Blackallac and head out.

I make my way through town and get on I-90 up to Spearfish City Park. I've stayed in the city park up there a couple of times and always enjoyed it. It is a little reminiscent of the old days in Sturgis. A lot of hardcore types from the old days. My intent is to find Dog.

Dog is an old-timer, one of the guys we used to call a "gray-beard" before we started getting gray ourselves. He's been coming to the rally since 1959. He's been staying at the same site for years at the Spearfish City Park. He shows up on the Wednesday before the rally to get it. He's an old club member from Fargo or something.

I pull around to his spot and he's already up and at 'em, as I had hoped, big pot of coffee at the ready. He's made hundreds of friends over the years and always plays the gracious host. Greetings done, we settle in. He asks, and I tell him where I ended up last night. A sly smiles forms under the wraparound shades, which I've never once seen him without. "Nothin' but bikes and clowns," he says. We laugh, each with his own vision in his head.

We sip coffee and B.S. for a while, enjoying an old friend-ship. Dog broke his back in a motorcycle accident about twenty years before. He was in the hospital for more than six months before they could even operate, but he was designing a new bike when he was still barely conscious. He rides a dresser with a modified side hack. His chair goes on to the side hack and he just rides on the seat. He's a riding fool, putting on tens of thou-sands of miles a year.

He is up for a ride up the canyon into Deadwood and for some breakfast, too. Deadwood canyon is one of the best rides in the Black Hills. Twists, turns, straighaways, with gorges and cliffs on either side. No one should visit the rally without making this ride.

We hit one of the casinos for breakfast. The food is so-so, but it is cheap and plentiful. Mostly buffets. We spend another hour talking and catching up. It doesn't seem like ten years have passed; we might have just seen each other last week at the local bar. Dog looks the part of an old fifties biker: longish slicked-back hair, perfectly combed plus the wraparound shades. He spends most of each year riding or sitting on the same corner on Main. I ask him if he ever gets tired of his rou-tine. "Naw," he shakes his head. "World's greatest freak show. Never get tired."

We split up after breakfast, he to his corner and me on to my sightseeing. I head out of Deadwood and up toward Lead and Highway 385. You can spend all day, or even days, in Deadwood if you want to, and I have in the past. There are caves and mines and casinos (which actually offer poker, a rarity) and one of the greatest bars on Earth, The Stockade. It is an outdoor bar and has been there since I don't know when. The owners actually allow folks to ride their bikes through it, which always brings about all kinds of cheers and hoisting of beers. It makes a biker feel like he owns the world to ride on through. It used to be the scene of lots of shenanigans—shirt lifting, etc.—and I don't know if it's changed or not. But I do have dozens of great memories of it.

Up toward Lead (pronounced Leed) I swing onto Highway 385. This is one of the roads that has earned the Black Hills

PAUL YAFFE AND HIS FLAME THROWER, SUNDANCE, WYOMING, 2003

FATHER AND SON STUNT RIDERS INSIDE A STEEL BALL, FULL THROTTLE SALOON, STURGIS, 2003

their reputation for riding. It is nothing but beautiful, tall, pencil-straight pines, smooth asphalt, sweeping turns, and elevation changes. I hum past the Silver City turn and Pactola Lake, and take a quick breather once I reach Sheridan Lake. This route is part of the old Gypsy tour. I stop at one of the lookouts that has walkways and bathroom facilities. The pines come almost to the shoreline all along the lake, and the water is a gorgeous blue. I find a spot a little ways off the walkway and pop a beer that I had stashed in my saddlebag in a nifty high-tech cooler.

Looking at the bikes in the lot, I notice a big difference from years past. It had been ten years since my last rally. Motorcycling had changed, and America had changed. There was a greater mix of bikes, to be sure. More Goldwings, and more of the Japanese cruisers that had become so popular, especially since the mid-nineties. I had gone to a motorcycle show back about that time. All of the major manufacturers were represented. I was looking at the new Harley models, wondering about a replacement for Blackallac.

The first time I brought her to Sturgis, she was a real head-turner. There weren't very many on the road like her. She was an Electra-Glide stripped down to bare bones and lowered, making one sleek machine. Most of the bikes back then were variations of the FXs (the Low Rider-type bikes), or the big full-dressed Electra-Glides with more stuff on them than you could count. Blackallac offered the long-distance comfort of a dresser, but had a retro look in her simplicity. A year or two later, Harley came out with the Roadking, which was a factory version of the bike I had spent countless hours and dollars creating. It soon became the most popular bike on the road and suddenly it became fashionable to ride a big bike again. The Roadking broke my heart.

One of the things that really struck me at that motorcycle show were the Japanese bikes. They looked every bit as stylish as the Harleys. I knew that their technology was often superior: Harley had only just put out a fuel-injected model a couple of years before, and the Japanese had been using it for years. Plus, the price was about five or six grand less than a Harley, without the two-to three-year waiting list. Maybe I was silly to put up with Harley's moneygrubbing, but there was something fundamental in me that couldn't ever make the switch to a Japanese bike. I never blamed others for making that decision; it was the smart thing to do.

Looking around the lot some more, I notice another change, which first struck me in town: the basic demographic switch that had occurred. The riders were all getting older. In the old days, say twenty years ago, it seemed that the average rider was in his late twenties or thirties. There were still plenty of graybeards around, and the retired touring types, but it was

essentially a younger guy's thing. Well, we had all gotten older for one thing, and the other major factor was that it had become stylish to ride. That led an awful lot of older guys, who could afford the payments on a $20,000 bike, to buy one, as they were still a hell of a lot cheaper than a Corvette, the traditional symbol or tool of the midlife crisis.

I realize: Who the hell am I to criticize? I am sitting here in the middle of my own midlife crisis, wondering what it all means, and if life has passed me by. I have to get out of here quick, so I jump on the bike and split, something that I have been doing all my life when my thoughts or a scene get too heavy. I hit her hard, heading down to Custer at a fast pace, passing a lot of bikes, and no doubt causing some consternation. I follow 385 down toward Custer, pause for a moment at the Crazy Horse memorial, and think, screw it, and continue on, not wanting to bother. At Custer, I head out of town and catch 89 up toward Sylvan Lake and the Needles Highway. This was also once part of the Gypsy tour. By heading down to Custer, I missed about six miles of the Needles, but there is still plenty left. The Needles is considered by many to be one of the premiere rides in America, though only twenty miles long. It is nothing but twists and turns, and has some really amazing tunnels dug right through solid rock. I slow my pace considerably, as the Needles needs to be respected, too dangerous to take lightly.

The slower pace and the amazing scenery have a calming effect on me, and by the time I hit Custer State Park, I am at peace again. I pick up 16A, which leads up to Keystone. It is a splendid ride in itself. I have put on some good miles and am anxious to hook up with some of the guys from home. There are a bunch coming in from my town.

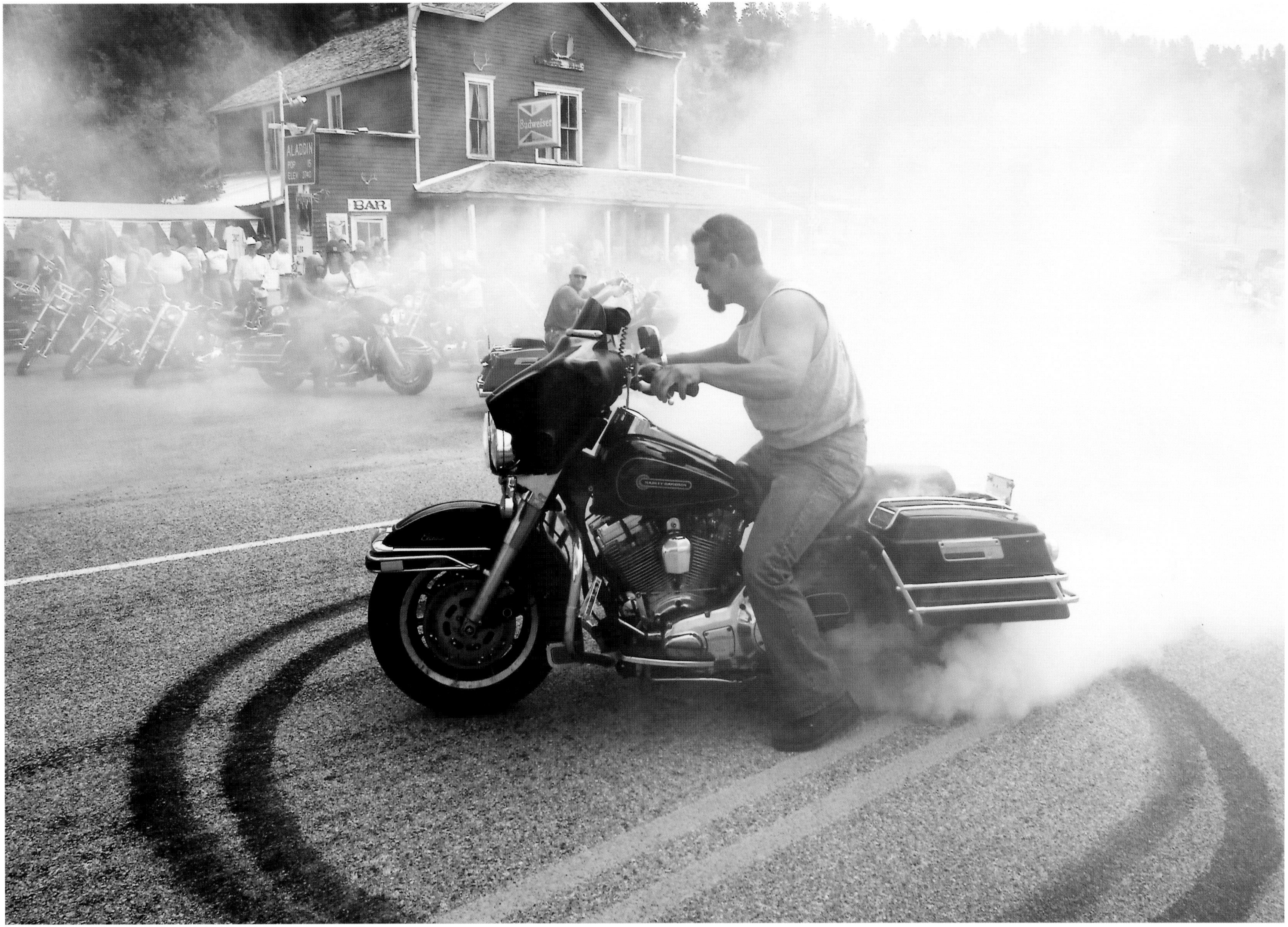

DOUGHNUTS, ALADDIN, WYOMING, 2002

Every year, the guy who owns the local gas station, Jim, acts as trail master and heads up an expedition to Sturgis and usually some other points out West. I figured I would know a lot of the guys and could beg a little space on the floor of someone's room.

Keystone is a really neat little town at the base of Mount Rushmore. It consists of one main street, from what I can tell, and is a really rustic, Western-looking place. It is like a mini Sturgis. Bikes parked all over the place and the boardwalks jammed with enthusiasts. It is mid-afternoon, and I figure a lot of people are stopping for an afternoon break, 'cause there doesn't seem to be enough space to accommodate all the folks I see. A bunch of Jim's crew are out front getting it together to go up to Rushmore to catch the sunset.

Following tradition, I jump in at the back of the formation. The road captain always leads with the president, in club situations. Then the other officers follow, with the rest behind in some order of seniority. The last guy is the sergeant at arms, who is in charge of getting everyone there safely. I am new to the group, so I follow toward the rear.

It is impossible to view Mount Rushmore without a feeling of the sacred. The Founding Fathers framed in a quintessential scene of American Western natural beauty. Experiencing the grit and determination to conquer the environment, which has been America's greatest achievement and led to some of her most shameful moments. With the sunset splashing the western side, I couldn't help but feel proud to be an American.

Many of Jim's crew were first-timers, so they were really lingering. I decide to head down the steps by the parking lot to observe the folks coming in. The contrast between the sun-

browned, leather-clad bikers and the pasty, baggy-short-wearing auto tourists is pretty humorous. But it occurs to me that many of the enthusiasts who are here for the week may well look like the auto tourists the other fifty weeks of the year.

Many of the old-time bikers have grown resentful of the Rich Urban Bikers (RUBs) who have become so much a part of the scene in recent years. Sometimes it seems that biker and lawyer have become synonymous. The old-timers feel like the victims of some form of identity theft.

Sturgis is about letting it all hang out, to relax and go wild for a few days, or to do whatever you want. To be the person you really are. So if a guy spends fifty-one weeks a year subduing his real self, then the vast majority of this life is a pretense? He is only real for one week a year?

Ask anyone why they are into motorcycling, and the answer invariably revolves around freedom. Motorcyclists feel they are free to be who they really are while on their motorcycles, free from the things that constrain them as people. They can drop all pretenses. No doubt that there are plenty of people who are trying to capture personas that they were attracted to when they where young, but too busy being "productive." They are pretending to be somebody. I think that the vast majority of people who ride are capturing the person they really are when allowed to be free. Sitting here at this historic site, one couldn't help but appreciate the idea of freedom.

A few years ago, I expressed the idea to Buddha, that the RUBs were stealing our identity. "If you where a plumber, could somebody steal your identity?" he asked.

"No, of course not," I shot back.

"Why not?" he replied.

"Because I would be a plumber due to what I know, because of my experiences."

Buddha smiled his enigmatic Buddha smile. "If someone puts on a plumber's clothes, are they a plumber?"

The point required no answer.

Bikers have always had the reputation for accepting people for who they are. In short, an ass is an ass and a standup person is a standup person. One needs to get lost and the other is welcome. It is about heart, loyalty, guts, and respect. A lawyer is as capable of having these qualities as a plumber. It isn't the bike that makes the biker, it is the person on it.

Subconsciously, I have been watching a lady sitting about five feet down the wall. Looking road-weary and alone. I strike up a conversation with her. Her name is Theresa, and she is from San Diego. She is a smallish woman, looking like she is Hispanic. She has ridden out here alone, when her old man's

vacation was canceled at the last minute. She rides a Sportster, which blows my mind. I haven't ridden anything with as much vibration and as little suspension on a long trip for many years. I even doubt my capacity to do a 5,000-mile trip on one. But she has done it by herself.

Turns out that Theresa is a federal agent, works the border, out in the boondocks. She has kicked down doors and has made some big busts. She is the one they bring in to do the interrogation. In talking to her, I can tell that she is a tough cop. Not hard, just tough. Theresa is a biker.

I ask her what she thinks of Mount Rushmore. "It is truly a wonder," she says, "but it is only half the story." I puzzle over that one. Finally, I ask her what she means. She asks me if I've been to the Crazy Horse memorial. I tell her that I haven't, and she simply says, "Go." I promise that I will, and walk back to where Blackallac is parked.

Jim's group is forming up. I hit him up for some floor space in his room, and of course he has no problem with it. I had no doubt. The next morning, I shower and pack up, anxious to get going. But I have two more stops before I leave town. Off of 16A, I get onto 244 and then head south on 385. Just as I start south, the rain starts.

Black Hills rainstorms come on quick and can get pretty fierce. Head pulled in to my chest, I get pelted by raindrops the size of marbles. My rain gear is buried in the saddlebags, so I just keep on. Rain is a part of traveling on a bike. If you stopped every time you got rained on you'd never get anywhere. Something I had noticed over recent years was the increasing use of the word comfortable, as in, "I'm not comfortable with that," or, "You're making me uncomfortable." Like being com-

fortable is a natural-born right. Those that lived on the road cherished comfort as something rare and unexpected.

Traveling by motorcycle is often about enduring discomfort. Rainstorms, uneven rocky ground to sleep on, and getting pelted by everything from bugs to hailstones. You shrug it off and just keep on. There is no guarantee of comfort on the road, and you learn not to expect it in life.

I turn into the memorial, lay down my fee, and head up to the main building. The parking lot is already full of bikes and vehicles of every description. As you walk in, the workers herd you right into one of the theaters. I don't know if I want to see the film, but I follow the crowd anyway.

The film they show centers around the creator of the memorial, Korczak Ziolkowski, and how he came to be the sculptor—or builder really—of the memorial. He was the son of Polish immigrants, and came from Boston. In 1939, he won first prize for sculpture at the New York World's Fair. Because of this, he came to the attention of Chief Standing Bear, of the Oglala Sioux. The Chief invited him out to South Dakota to lay a plan

on him. Anyone might say a crazy plan. The Chief wanted to build a memorial out of a mountain. A memorial to Crazy Horse, the famous Sioux warrior.

Crazy Horse was one of the engineers of Custer's defeat and had refused to live on one of the Native American reservations. Back in 1868, a major treaty was signed, giving the Black Hills to the Native Americans, "as long as the rivers flowed and the grass growed," or some such lie. Once gold was discovered, all bets were off, and the government not only let settlers take the Black Hills, but stuffed the Sioux onto reservations and starved them to death. With their lands confiscated, some smart-ass white man asked Crazy Horse, "Where are your lands now?" Crazy Horse replied, "My lands are where my dead lie buried." This answer may have sent a chill down the white guy's spine, as it not only addressed the Native American ancestors, but also the dead that were to come in the battles to follow.

About a decade later, Crazy Horse was killed by a white man who stabbed him in the back—such an obvious metaphor, I even hesitate to mention it. Crazy Horse is memorialized as an American hero, but a hero of the other America, and the America of others. As much of a freedom fighter as any other American, but historically ignored or reviled by mainstream America. The white America, the America represented by the four heads on Rushmore.

Six years after being approached, and after getting wounded in the Pacific during WWII, Ziolkowski decided to take on the Crazy Horse project. He made a 1/300-scale model of his intentions, and then predicted that it would take thirty years and five million dollars to complete. His final outcome would be many times the size of Rushmore.

He started to shape the mountain in 1947. Pictures reveal that when he came to South Dakota for the first time, he looked like an East Coast square wearing an outfit that looks like an East Coast idea of something from the West. As Ziolkowski shaped the mountain, he began to look like the West was shaping him. He wore a working man's clothes, grew a full, bushy beard, and wore a beaten-up old cowboy hat.

As the years went on, it became apparent that Ziolkowski grossly underestimated his task. By 1981, over seven million tons of rock had been removed, and the face was not even complete. He was careful to preserve his many drawing and plans in the hope that the work will carry on after his death. He died in 1982, at age seventy-eight. He was memorialized as a man of legends, dreams, visions, and greatness. As well as an incomplete project, Ziolkowski left behind a dedicated wife and ten children, eight of whom decided to carry on the dream, along with his wife. In 1998, fifty years after the first Black Hills Motor Classic, the finished face was revealed to the crowd of thousands who gathered to celebrate.

In a show of great independence, Ziolkowski wanted the project to be financially self-sufficient. He declined millions and millions of dollars in grant money, preferring instead to raise the funds from visitors and donors. There is no estimate of when the memorial will be finished; the body and horse are undone. It depends on things like finances and the weather. The Crazy Horse memorial is actually a memorial to two men, one a freedom fighter and the other man with a giant vision, dedicating his life to memorializing the freedom fighter, and the other America.

As I prowl around the huge complex, my mind turns to my definition of spirituality—simply the awareness of the vast greatness that exists outside yourself—and realize what a spiritual place this is. It forces one to see that vast greatness that exists all around you. Sometimes in us, and sometimes outside us, in the physical world. And maybe that's what Sturgis is really about, forcing you to see the greatness all around you, outside of yourself, and what motorcycling is really about.

I have one more stop to hit before I head back east. I turn toward Rapid and head up 234 to Nemo and then take 135, Vanocker Canyon Road, back into Sturgis. This back way is relatively lightly traveled and was one of the roads that the original Gypsies often favored. I pull into Sturgis and come to a stop in front of an indistinguishable ranch house in the middle of a quiet neighborhood. This is the home of Pearl and the late Pappy Hoel. I feel driven to pay my respects to this pioneer of the rally.

As I walk up to the front door, Pearl comes out to meet me.

"Are you the young man that called this morning?"

"Yes ma'am, I am." I want to meet a real-life pioneer. We walk around to the backyard, fenced in and set up for socializing, with tables and chairs everywhere. As we sit, I have an opportunity to study her face. At ninety-seven, her face bears many lines, the kind of lines that can be beautiful on an old, experienced face. And she has perfectly clear, blue eyes that look right at you. Thin and straight as an arrow. I feel as if I am in the presence of a tribal elder. She tells me she is the only woman who has been to every rally. I ask her if she used to ride with Pappy, and she replies that she wishes she had a nickel for every mile she's ridden. Through Canada and around the West.

She tells me of how they traveled to the Mayo Clinic in Minnesota to have her neck examined. The doctor, upon meeting

PAUL COX FLYING DOWN HIGHWAY 79 NEAR BEAR BUTTE, STURGIS, 2003

her, asked how she had gotten there. When she told him by motorcycle, he told her to go home, she didn't need any help. We laugh, and she tells me of growing up in the area, having lived here for about ninety years. She had been the teacher at a one-room schoolhouse, and a project-money inspector during "the dirty thirties." Her job was to inspect the farms and ranches, making sure that the government project money was getting spent. But she spent much of her time distributing the meat that the cattlemen gave her to help out the families that were going without. "That's how it was, you just helped each other out." To me this communalism seems a vital part of the West.

She describes the early years of the rally, the work she and Pappy put in to see their dream come true, mostly for the satisfaction of doing something to promote the sport they loved and the town they loved.

She met Pappy while she was a schoolteacher, drawn to the independent young man, a biker of the day, despite being the proper schoolteacher. And spent a lifetime with him, supporting his dreams, and welcoming the multitude of friends he always brought around. Happy to feed a few extra for dinner or breakfast.

She talks of Pappy's unusual talent for making friends of anybody, even the German prisoners of war during WWII, using their mechanical abilities to tune up the cavalry's motorcycles.

She talks in glowing terms of the racers who used to hang around the shop during the rally, competitors and rivals working side by side. "They were just like a bunch of kids that all liked to play the same game. Everybody got along."

She describes the year that the sheriff came to Pappy, telling him that the rally might have to be shut down because a group of outlaw bikers were coming. Pappy promised to handle it. When the day came, he met them outside of town. He walked up to the leader and told him, "You guys are as welcome as anyone else. But you start any trouble, and you'll find out we mean business." The outlaws proceeded into town, and there wasn't a bit of trouble. They respected the man too much.

When I ask about other trouble over the years, she tells me that there never has been much of anything. "You'd see more in a place like Rapid City on any weekend. It's like Clarence [Pappy] always said, you could have a bunch of preachers here for a weekend, and there'd still be a couple rotten apples. It just goes to show you—"

I wait for her to finish, but she doesn't. And I think about what it was to show. I think about stereotypes. But in all, her stories seems to have a central theme: True individuals brought together working for love and pure enjoyment. Looking to give a helping hand. And what it means to have individuals like this, from the past, and how it forms today.

After an hour or so, I tell her that I have to get going, that I have a long ride home. She walks me out to my bike, holding my jacket for me while I get on. When I start my bike up and put the jacket on, she just looks me square in the eye, and says, "Make sure you have a good time." I thank her and head out of the town, to the interstate.

I join the throngs of motorcycles heading east. Some ridden by bikers, some by enthusiasts. It doesn't really matter which is the case. Everyone is doing their own thing, and that is okay. I opt to make the Badlands Loop. I love the Badlands Loop. So uniform and even scary-looking at a casual glance. So deep and concentric upon study.

Sturgis has changed over the years, as have I. I marvel that I had ever expected any different. I set out on this trip looking for the old times, looking for the old me, as have I. Feeling lost. But in talking to that old woman, who has lived more than twice as long as I have, I have come to think about the spirit of things, about spirits in general.

A spirit is the essence of a thing, but it is also the memory of things. When we feel like spirits inhabit a place, we are sensing that essence and reliving those memories. On this journey to Sturgis, I discovered its essence and lived the memory of it from the beginning until this moment. Having done so, I relived the memories of my own personal journey and discovered the essence of who I was. And I still have a long way to go.

BIBLIOGRAPHY:

Edeburn, Carl. *Sturgis: The Story of the Rally*. South Dakota: Dimensions Press, 2003.

Eliot, T.S. "Burnt Norton" *Four Quartets*. London: The Folio Society, 1968.

Pirsig, Robert. *Zen and the Art of Motorcycle Maintenance*. New York: William Morrow and Company, 1984.

Thompson, Hunter S. *Hells Angels: The Strange and Terrible Saga of the Outlaw Motorcycle Gang*. New York: Ballantine Books, 1966.